Mesila's

Mesivta Program

Educator's Guide

MESILA

Providing the Path to Financial Stability

© 2016
Mesila's Mesivta Program - Educator's Guide

ISBN 978-1-941902-21-9

Authored by:
Malky Heimowitz
and Batya Weinberg

Questions or comments may be sent to:

Mesila
P.O.B. 57116
Jerusalem 9157002, Israel
Tel: +972.2.500.0475
Fax: +972.2.500.0478
info@mesila.org
www.mesila.org
Reg. Amuta No. 580361236
Tax ID No. 11-3597720

Mesila Education Division

Core Values and Concepts

Some of the values and underlying ideas brought across by our curriculum are:

Bitachon and Hishtadlus

- **A believing Jew's attitude towards finance:** Striking the Torah-mandated balance between *bitachon* and *hishtadlus*.
- **Responsibility:** Realizing that the Torah obligates us to take reasonable measures to ensure our financial stability and future.

Financial Management

- **Awareness and control:** Meticulous recording of financial data brings an awareness and control, allowing us to make sensible decisions.
- **Planning ahead:** If you fail to plan, you plan to fail.
- **Paying attention to details:** Little things add up very quickly; attention to detail can make the difference between success and failure.

Money and Materialism

- **Money is a means only:** Material gain is not an end in itself, but rather a tool to enable the effective implementation of Torah values.
- **Defining satisfaction:** Learning to identify satisfaction with values, relationships, and accomplishments, irrelevant of size of bank account.
- **Resisting materialism:** Learning to resist advertising lures and excessive emphasis on material goods.
- **Delayed gratification:** Waiting for things we really want brings emotional and material dividends.
- **Thinking independently:** What others have or need is not necessarily what I have or need – avoiding comparisons.

Responsibility to Others

- **Integrity:** Stringent honesty in money matters and in all areas, big and small.
- **Respecting property:** Accepting boundaries and respecting the property of others as well as our own.
- ***Chessed* and *tzedakah*:** Appreciating that our money is entrusted to us to share with others.
- **Positive peer pressure:** Recognizing that our actions impact what others will do and using that realization to trigger positive change.

Prioritizing

- **Needs and wants:** Differentiating between needs and wants: Needs become stronger with time, while wants wane.
- **Balancing needs and wants:** Defining the financial goal as ensuring that we have everything we need and some of what we want.
- **Importance of prioritizing:** Ranking demands and desires and balancing time, energy, and money according to thought-out priorities.

החוברת טעונה גניזה
Parts of this publication may require *genizah*.
Please do not discard.

Table of Contents

Units

Student Resources

Assignments

Appendix

מסילתם של גדולי ישראל

MESILA
Providing The Path to Financial Stability

מסילה
לכלכלה נבונה

מרן פוסק הדור הגרי"ש אלישיב זצוק"ל

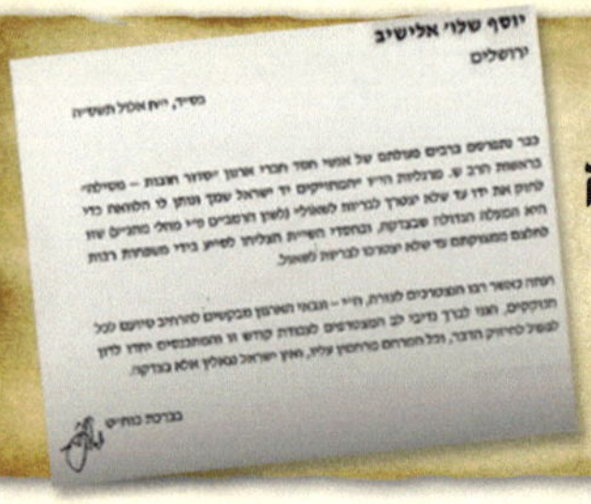

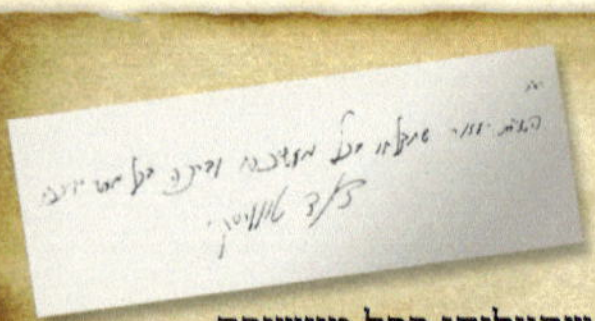

"השי"ת יעזור שתצליחו בכל מעשיכם וברכה בכל מעשי ידיכם".

כ"ק האדמו"ר מרחמסטריווקא שליט"א

מרן פוסק הדור הגר"ש הלוי ואזנר זצוק"ל

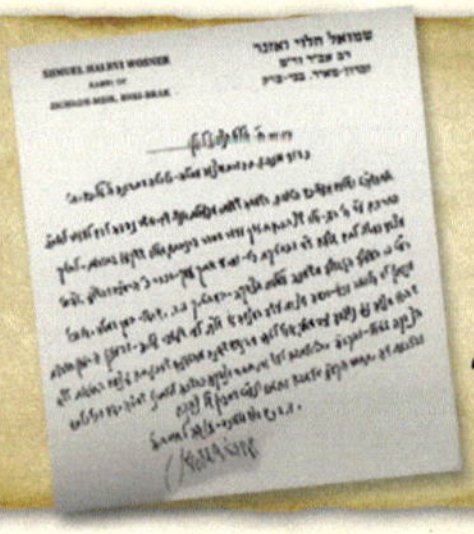

"לכל העוסקים והמסייעים והתורמים שיבורכו בברכת ברכה והצלחה וסייעתא דשמיא וכל הברכות של גדולי הדור יחולו עליהם".

הצדיק רבי דוד אבוחצירא שליט"א

כ"ק האדמו"ר מתולדות אהרן שליט"א

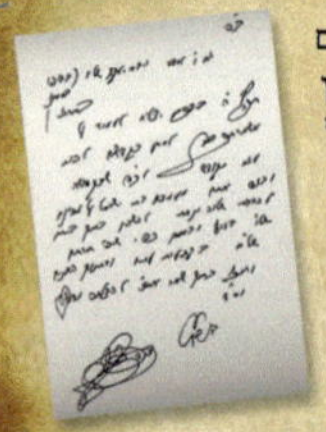

יום ו' לסדר ויבא יעקב שלם (בגופו בממונו בתרתי) חפץ ה' בידכם יצליח לעמוד על משמרתכם לסייע בקדשים להיות עזר מקודש לכ"ד שבקדושה ובזה אתם מעמידים בתי ישראל על מכונם להרבות שלוה ונחת להשכין בתוך ביתם שלו' בגוף ובממון כדי שיהי' תורתם שלם בקביעות עתים ובחינוך הבנים ותזכו בתוך שאר אחב"י להצלחה מרובה וס"ד דוש"ט.

גאב"ד רבי יצחק טובי' ווייס שליט"א

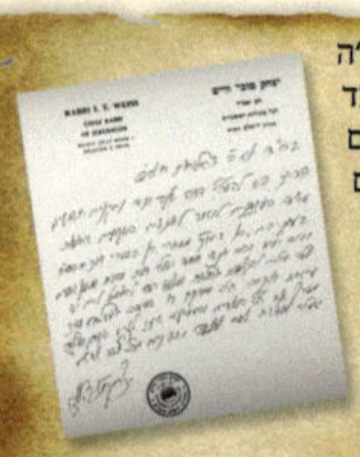

בס"ד יום ה' דסליחות תשס"ה הריני בא להמליץ בזה בעד ועד עסקנים חשובים מאד העוסקים לעזור לאנשים השקועים בחובות בעסקיהם, הן ביעוץ מסחרי הן בשארי דרכים כגמ"ח ועוד ועוד והם אנשי חסד ובעלי דעת ידועים ומובן שדברים אלה עולים להוצאות גדולות, ומצוה רבה להושיט להם יד עוזרת ולקיים בזה והחזקת ידו במידה גדולה והריני מברך את כל העוזרים והמסייעים שיזכו לשפע ברכה והצלחה במילוי משאלות לבם לטובה ורב נחת מכל יוצ"ח אכי"ר.

כ"ק האדמו"ר מדושינסקיא שליט"א

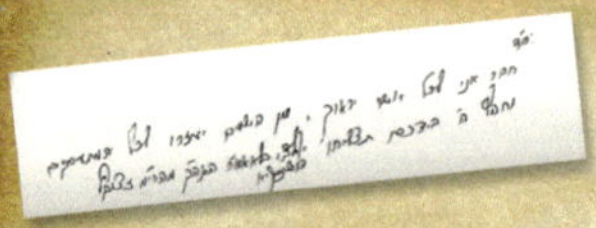

חבר אני לכל אשר יראוך, מן השמים יעזרו לכל המתעסקים וחפץ ה' בידכם תצליחו.
יום ב', בלאאמו"ר הגה"ק מהרי"מ זצוק"ל דושינסקיא

הגאון רבי שמאי קהת הכהן גראס שליט"א

חיים על פי עקרונות 'מסילה' הם חיי תורה אמיתיים. על כן צריכים להכיר טובה עצומה לארגון "מסילה", שנציגיו היקרים מתעדכנים כל הזמן בידע מקצועי ומתודרכים על ידי אנשי מקצוע. ומשקיעים זמן יקר וכוחות נפש אדירים לטיפול בבעיותיהם של אחרים. אברכים יקרים אלו המסייעים למשפחות לבנות את עצמן בגשמיות, מציעים להן בעצם חיי איכות רוחניים. אין איפוא כל פלא בכך, ששומעים על ראשי משפחות שהחלו לחיות על פי עקרונות "מסילה" והפסיקו לחפש כל העת מקורות לגלגול חובות, ובד בבד החלו גם ליטול חלק בשיעורי תורה, הוסיפו בקיום מצוות והצליחו יותר בחינוך צאצאיהם שיחי'. ברכותי לארגון "מסילה"; המשיכו לעסוק במלאכת הקודש שלכם באמונה ובמסירות, וברכת שמים תחול על ראשכם, להחדיר בכלל ישראל חיים של תורה, חיים של פרנסה, חיים של אהבת תורה ויראת שמים.

MESILA
Providing The Path to Financial Stability

מסילתם של גדולי ישראל

מסילה
לכלכלה נבונה

בס"ד

לכבוד
יראי ה' וחושבי שמו
די בכל אתר ואתר

יצו ה' אתכם את הברכה, החיים והשלום.

בשנה שחלפה היינו עדים, לצערנו, לקריסת מערכות כלכלית שעדיין אין רואים את סופה. אנשים רבים, ביניהם יראים ושלמים איבדו את ממונם בענין רע זה. אין ספק כי אחד הגורמים העיקריים לכך הוא האשראי המיותר שאיפשר לאנשים לבצע עיסקאות שגויות בכסף לא להם. גורם נוסף הוא תרבות הצריכה שלשמה אנשים מוציאים הרבה מעבר ליכולתם. כולנו מייחלים ומקוים שיפתח ה' לנו את אוצרו הטוב לתת רוב טובה לעם קדוש, ולוואי שלא ינזקו חלילה אחב"י, בכל מושבותם, לא בגופם ולא בממונם, ושלא יצטרכו זה לזה ולא לעם אחר.

ע"מ לזכות לכל הנ"ל נדרש מאתנו להתנהג בהתאם - יש לזכור כי בחובתו של יהודי עלי אדמות נכלל גם החיוב לנהוג באחריות, בזהירות וביושר, בענייני ממון, בכספו וכ"ש בכספם של אחרים. וכמו בשאר דברים, **אף זו תורה היא, וללימוד היא צריכה, ויש להכיר את הכללים כדי לדעת להתנהג כראוי וכיאות ובלא להכשל ולהכשיל.**

והנה, זה כמה שנים שקיים ופועל באה"ק ארגון החסד "מסילה לכלכלה נבונה", שראשיו ומייסדיו הי"ו שמו לנגד עיניהם את המטרה החשובה, להביא לכל בית בישראל את דרך ההתנהגות הכלכלית הנכונה והישרה עפ"י התורה וההלכה. ארגון מסילה, מקיים מערך ארצי של מאות יועצים מתנדבים המדריכים משפחות ועסקים ליציבות כלכלית באופן פרטי ולאורך זמן.

תשרי תש"ע

לאחרונה החל מסילה גם בפעילות הסברה והדרכה לחתנים ובנות סמינר כיצד לנהל את משק הבית והוצאותיו בדרך הנכונה, כדי להקדים רפואה למכה ולמנוע מראש ככל הניתן קשיים כספיים, למען יהיו הבתים הנבנים בישראל מבוססים על יסודות איתנים ומוצקים.

במשך השנים זכה ארגון מסילה וצוות המתנדבים הפועלים בשורותיו, להציב מאות משפחות ועסקים, ביניהם גם כאלו שהיו שקועים בקשיים עמוקים, על דרך הכלכלה הנבונה, ובכך להביאם לחיים של שלוות הנפש רגיעה ויישוה"ד המאפשרים לאדם להתמסר לחובותיו האמיתיים בעולמו.

בשל החשיבות הרבה של הנושא, ממליצים אנו לכל אחד ואחד להטות אוזן לדברים, ולהשתדל ללמוד את נושא ניהול כלכלת הבית, ויהי זה בבחי' השתדלות שתעזור בס"ד לחסוך צער ועגמ"נ בעתיד. כמו כן, מי שמרגיש בעצמו כי חננו השי"ת בכשרון ויכולת להבין את הדבר לעומקו, ונשאו לבו לתרום מזמנו ולהתנדב בשורות הארגון, יוכל לאחר הכשרה יסודית לזכות בס"ד להעלות משפחות על דרך המלך, לחיים של אושר ושלוה.

למותר לציין כי הכוונת הפעילות, הפרסום וסדנאות ההדרכה, הכשרת המתנדבים והחזקת עשרות הסניפים עולים כסף רב. **התורם למטרה נעלה זו של ליווי וייעוץ למשפחות בטרם התמוטטות זוכה להמנות על מקיימי מצוות צדקה בדרגה הגבוהה ביותר**, כמבואר ברמב"ם ובפוסקים שהמחזיק ידי ישראל עד שלא יצטרך לבריות היא המעלה שאין למעלה הימנה, **וקונה לו בזה זכות גדולה עד מאד, שתעמוד לימינו בס"ד לשנה טובה ומבורכת, ולשפע ברכה והצלחה בכל אשר יפנה.**

נפתלי נוסבוים
נתן הכהן קופשיץ
מנחם מנדל הכהן שפרן

סמכה דעתינו ונאמנים עלינו הרה"ג שליט"א המכוונים את פעילות ארגון מסילה, ומצטרפים אנו לדבריהם על גודל חשיבות ונחיצות הענין. ברור שיש לכל יר"ש לחשב היטב הליכותיו בענייני ממון וכספים, כי רבה המכשלה ושכיח הזיקא לפני מי שאינו מתבונן כראוי. יה"ר שיתברכו כל העוסקים והמסייעים ממקור הברכות לשנה טובה ומבורכת בכל מילי דמיטב בגו"ר.

דבר חשוב הוא למשפחות אלו והארגון כל מעשיהם לש"ש.

חיים קנייבסקי
ג.א. מצטרף א.ל.שטיינמן
ניסים קרליץ
מיכל יהודה ליפקוביץ

הנני מכיר את העסקנים החשובים שיחיו ומברך את העוסקים והמסייעים בכל מילי דמיטב.

בעה"ח ישראל בהה"צ מויזניץ שליט"א

נוכחתי לדעת עד היכן חשובה העבודה שארגון מסילה עוסקת בה, חסד גדול עם הציבור ועם יחידים להדריכם בנתיבות החיים. יה"ר שתשרה שכינה במעשי ידיהם.

יעקב פרלוב

Introduction

An Ounce of Prevention

The Mesila Financial Literacy Course is designed to give young people the tools to manage their finances correctly and avoid financial pitfalls and missteps. In Mesila's many years of working with families to achieve financial stability, we have seen that much financial stress and heartache can be avoided with preventative financial education.

As more and more U.S. states are beginning to require personal finance courses in high schools, many Jewish schools are facing a unique dilemma: on the one hand, we wish to equip our students with the tools, skills, and knowledge they will require in order to be financially literate and achieve financial stability; on the other hand, this information is often at odds - overtly or subtly - with the educational values that Torah institutions promote. To choose a few examples out of many:

• **Consumerism:** In the secular world, encouraging people to purchase more is considered beneficial, since it stimulates the economy. In our worldview, however, consumerism is dangerous, because it leads to an emphasis on the material, at the expense of the spiritual.

• **Wealth:** Building wealth is probably the single most important goal of all secular financial literacy education. As Torah Jews, we understand that money is merely a means to an end, and that we cannot encourage building wealth as a goal unto itself.

• **Interest, loans, life insurance:** These are some areas of finance that involve serious halachic issues. In presenting these topics, teachers have to be extremely sensitive to the halachic ramifications. That is why, for instance, Mesila's financial literacy course includes the full text of a heter iska for study.

The six units that comprise the Mesila Financial Literacy Course focus primarily on the attitudes and skills necessary for personal financial management. Additional technical information (on subjects such as insurance and risk management, retirement and estate planning, and taxes) may be supplemented by the teacher using the recommended textbook, Personal Finance (tenth edition) by Jack R. Kapoor, Les R. Dlabay and Robert J. Hughes (McGraw-Hill/Irwin 2012).

The Teachers' Guide provides a clear and concise six-unit course outline that covers all important points, while leaving the teacher ample room for creativity and innovation in presenting the material.

Please note the following elements present in the Guide:

- **Course outline:** Each unit addresses one major area of financial literacy, with a sidebar on the first page summarizing the unit's goals. The body of the unit presents the issues, solutions and underlying principles in bullet list form.

- **Mekoros:** Included are many relevant Torah sources. Emphasized is that money is an inseparable part of Torah living governed by halacha and haskafah.

- **Reference to Student Text material:** At key points in each unit, reference is made to student resources This material should not be regarded as "extra enrichment," but rather as crucial information to round out the unit.

- **Powerpoint Presentations:** A number of subjects, such as attitudes and credit card use, are colorfully presented in visual form via well-designed video presentations. These serve as an excellent basis for class discussion.

- **Unit with Assignments:** The assignments have proven to be highly effective in cementing the concepts that were covered. These may be assigned as individual or group work, or creatively presented in interactive form, such as a panel discussion or even a student fair.

- **Springboards for discussion:** At some junctures in the Teachers' Guide, suggestions appear for topics that can rouse lively debate. The teacher may choose from these the ones most suitable for the class.

In consideration of the unique needs and sensitivities of our students, Mesila has developed a financial literacy course that teaches the relevant material through the prism of Torah hashkafah and takes into account the realities and challenges students will face. We wish to give special thanks to Mrs. T. Lichtenstein of Yerushalayim for her invaluable assistance and input in the preparation of this course.

We welcome suggestions, questions, and other feedback. Feel free to contact us at info@mesila.org.

Mesila Education Division

Part 1:

Units

Unit 1

Financial Stability

Goals:

- To understand what financial stability is and why it's important
- To identify obstacles to financial stability
- To examine spending habits and their impact on financial stability
- To learn how to prioritize and make financially sound decisions
- To understand the concepts of opportunity cost and the time value of money.
- To identify mistaken attitudes toward money and replace them with healthy attitudes.

Financial stability is the ability to handle your financial obligations in a way that contributes positively to other areas of your life. If you are financially stable, then your finances should enhance – not detract from – your health, your relationships, your quality of life, your peace of mind, and your ability to reach your life goals. This definition of financial stability views money as a tool, a means to a higher end, rather than as an end unto itself.

A. Introduction to Financial Stability

1) Financial stability - standard definition: Having adequate income to cover your expenses, both present and future.

2) Mesila's definition: Financial stability is the ability to handle your financial obligations in a way that contributes positively to other areas of your life. If you are financially stable, then your finances should enhance - not detract from - your health, your relationships, your quality of life, your peace of mind, and your ability to reach your life goals. This definition of financial stability views money as a tool, a means to a higher end, rather than as an end unto itself.

3) Difference between the two definitions: Do we equate success with how much money we have, or with how well we live with what we have?

4) Financial instability is what happens when finances become a source of anxiety, difficulty, or strife.

5) Financial stability is not a function of how much money you have. There are millionaires who suffer from terrible financial instability, because money is a source of tension and conflict in their lives, and there are low-income families who are models of financial stability, because they manage well with what they have and lead productive, happy lives despite their meager means.

6) Obstacles to financial stability:

   There are a number of reasons why a family might experience financial difficulty:

   a) Low income: Many families simply do not earn enough money to cover basic living costs.

   b) High standard of living: Some families have enough money to cover basic living costs, but spend more than they have in order to live on a higher standard. This might be due to social pressure, a desire to impress others, a desire for comfort or convenience, or habits ingrained from childhood..

   c) A one-time expense: A family might experience financial difficulty because of a large one-time expense such as buying a home, the birth of a child, a wedding, or a medical procedure.

   d) Reduction of income: Unemployment, a pay cut, or a family business that is doing poorly can cause a severe reduction in a family's income, leading to financial difficulty.

   e) Jumbled business and personal finances: When business finances are mixed up with personal finances - i.e., the business owner's salary is used to pay business debts, while the profits of the business are used to pay for the family's expenditures - finances become chaotic. Not knowing which funds need to stay in the business and which funds belong to the family can cause the financial collapse of the business, the family, or both.

   f) Misplaced piety: Some people misunderstand the concept of *bitachon* and say "Hashem will help" when proactive measures are called for.

   g) Carelessness: A cavalier attitude to money is a significant contributing factor, and at times the only factor, in many cases of financial difficulty. A careless attitude towards money manifests itself in superficial management of finances and irresponsible financial behavior, such as spending or investing money wantonly without considering the ramifications or risks. People with this attitude tend to think in terms of profit, and not in terms of stability. They see lack of money as a temporary, confined problem, and try to find instant solutions instead of working hard and planning for the long-term.

h) Gambling and spending addictions: Like other addictions, gambling and spending addictions are terribly destructive, and require professional intervention. Gamblers and compulsive spenders can squander huge amounts of money and land their families in serious financial trouble.

- Student Resource no. 1: **Mesila's Guidelines for Financial Stability and Accompanying Exercise**

These 47 points, culled from Mesila's many years of experience counseling families and businesses, constitute a succinct overview of the elements of financial stability.

B. Financial Stability in Practical Terms

Having everything you need and some of what you want.

1. "Everything you need"

a) A person has to be aware of what he/she needs and wants in order to function and thrive. This is the basis of establishing spending priorities.

b) Needs are subjective, based on the following factors:

(1) Society (Location/Time): Your needs are determined, to a large extent, by the place and time you live in.

(a) If you live in Eretz Yisrael, you might consider a car a luxury. If you live in North America, you might consider a second car a necessity.

(b) To a person who was born in the 1940s, a cell phone is a nice thing to have, but it's possible to manage without it, too. To a person born in the 1990s, a cell phone might be an absolute necessity.

(c) A person's society also determines what is considered wealth. For example:

- Rothschild rode in a horse and buggy and had no indoor plumbing or air conditioning - so why did he feel like Rothschild and we don't?
- A researcher said that the time of his life when he felt the richest was when he was on assignment in Africa and his hut had a thatched roof while the other huts had simpler roofs.

(2) **Personality:** People have different physical needs and sensitivities.

(a) Some people can live on tuna sandwiches happily; they might not understand someone else's need to eat out when there's nothing in the fridge

(b) Some people can sleep on any type of bed; to them, it seems odd that people would invest in expensive mattresses or bedding

(3) **Upbringing & Conditioning:** If someone is brought up with more, they might need more than others. This reality is also reflected in halachah: One is obligated to give charity according to the lifestyle to which the needy person is accustomed, not according to an objective standard of need, because needs are not objective.

(4) **Circumstances:** Different circumstances give rise to different needs

(a) Size/age of family: A large family might need a larger house or car. A young family might need a lot of babysitting.

(b) Work schedule: A mother who is working might take more household help or buy readymade food.

(c) Illness or disability: When people are not well, they may need treatments, therapies, or various types of help.

c) Student Resource no. 2: **Maslow's Hierarchy of Needs**

There are different categories of needs, expressed as a pyramid in Maslow's Hierarchy of Needs: Physiological, safety, love/belonging, esteem, self-actualization. When establishing spending priorities, all of these needs have to be taken into account. It is important to realize, however, that not all needs can be met with money.

2. "Some of what you want"

a) It is important to have some of what you want (but not **everything** you want) because practically speaking, a person cannot function optimally unless his needs are met and he also has a bit extra that is not absolutely necessary, so that he doesn't feel suffocated or deprived.

b) There is no limit to what a person can want. Therefore, it's important to think through your wants before deciding to indulge one, because having one thing you want often comes at the expense of something you want more. *(See next page - opportunity cost)*

Student Resource no. 3: **Fifteen Hundred Dollar Eye Glasses**

3. Differentiating between needs and wants

How do we know whether something is a need or a want?

- Needs: Generally, if needs are unmet, they become more intense and lead to feelings of deprivation.
- Wants: Generally, if we deny ourselves something we want, we exercise and strengthen our self-control and self-discipline muscles.
  Example: If a person is hungry and does not yield to the urge to eat, he will only become hungrier, because he has a real need for food. But if a person wants chocolate and does not give in to the urge, eventually his desire for chocolate will abate and it will become easier for him to resist the temptation.
- Test for differentiating between needs and wants: Wait a while and see - does the desire intensify or weaken with time? Needs tend to intensify with time and wants tend to abate.

Discussion: When standard of living rises, causing luxuries ("wants") to become necessities ("needs"), does that make people happier or less content? Give examples of wants that have become needs. Note: The incidence of depression is much higher in wealthy countries.

4. Establishing spending priorities

- What does "I can't afford it" mean? Sometimes it means you don't have the money; sometimes it means it's not important to you.
- Opportunity cost
  1. Dictionary definition: Cost in terms of foregoing alternatives
  2. Practical definition: If I buy this, I can't buy that
  3. The Time/Energy/Money Triangle:
     Human beings have three main types of resources: time, energy, and money. Every action you take and every pursuit in which you engage will require a balance of the three. Often, you can save money by expending more time or energy, or you can conserve time or energy by spending money.

  Discussion: How do you arrange your daily schedule to fit in everything you want to do while maximizing your resources? Remember: Your money is limited. Your physical energy is limited. Your time is limited. All three need to be budgeted carefully so that you can get the most out of your life.

PowerPoint presentation:

Attitudes to Money

Many financial problems stem from flawed attitudes towards money. So much unnecessary anguish comes from misguided reasoning, which can be remedied with a conscious shift in perspective. Adopting correct, Torah-based attitudes can enable people to manage their finances wisely and avoid countless financial difficulties.

5. Marshmallow Experiment

In the 1960s, psychologist Walter Mischel conducted the famous Marshmallow Temptation Study among four-year-olds. In this experiment, Mischel presented each child with a marshmallow.

He then told the child that he or she could either eat the marshmallow immediately, or wait and get an additional marshmallow as a reward.

As anticipated, some children yielded to the temptation and some others withstood it. Walter Mischel followed the progress of these children, monitored their school records, and surveyed and interviewed their teachers and parents until the students reached age 18.

Results

What he found has significant implications for education: children who had resisted the marshmallow temptation turned out to be more successful and emotionally balanced than those who had given into the temptation.

They were better-adjusted and more dependable.

More specifically, children who could delay gratification scored 250 points higher on the Scholastic Aptitude Test, worked well under pressure and when in groups, were significantly more confident, and possessed a number of other positive traits and habits.

a) It is important to emphasize that even though there are those who are born with a tendency for more restraint, the possibilities of what a person can achieve are endless, and it is our job in life to overcome negative character traits.

b) When it comes to spending money in particular, the benefits of delaying gratification, rather than going for immediate - and often only perceived - reward, are tangible. When we give our mind control over our emotions in this realm, we feel the results in all areas of our lives.

Student Resource no. 4: **This is Your Brain on Easy Credit**

6. Financial Stability: For the Poor, the Rich, And the In-Between

כל ענייני העולם בין לטוב בין (למוטב) לרע הנה הם נסיונות לאדם, העוני מצד אחד והעושר מצד אחד כענין שאמר שלמה (משלי ל): פן אשבע וכחשתי ואמרתי מי ה', ופן אורש וגנבתי וכו'.

All matters of the world, whether good or bad, are challenges for a person – poverty on one hand, and wealth on the other hand, as Shlomo HaMelech said, "Lest I become satiated and I deny and say, 'Who is Hashem?' and lest I become impoverished and steal." (Mesilas Yesharim, ch. 1)

Question: *What if you have a lot of money? Do you still need to pay attention to your finances? What if your parents don't limit your spending? Do you still need to learn about how to achieve financial stability?*

Answer: YES!

Why?

Three reasons why people who can afford to buy whatever they want still need to develop healthy financial habits:

REASON #1:

Lifestyle demands continuously expand to exceed income.

Parkinson's Law states that work expands to fill the time, and the same is true of money. Expenses rise to meet income, because when funds are available, they find a destination. And when people's income rises, their needs rise, too - but their needs usually rise more than their income. So no matter how much money you have, you always need more, and the more money you have, the more you're going to spend.

Example:

Say you're earning $80,000 a year now, and you think you need $100,000. Say you managed somehow to increase your income from $80,000 to $100,000. What would happen? Would you find that all of your financial problems would be solved? From Mesila's experience, we'd guess that what would probably happen is that your expenses would rise to match and exceed your income. We project that if you were earning $100,000, your expenses would rise to $125,000. All told, you would be worse off than you are now - now, you only need an extra $20,000, not $25,000.

Let's take this a step further and project what would happen if you would be earning only $60,000 now. Would you still need $100,000 to live on? Probably not. If you were earning $60,000, our guess is that you would say that you need less than the $80,000 you are currently earning.

We don't need all this scientific reasoning, because Chazal already expressed this when they said: יש לו מנה רוצה מאתיים

> אין אדם יוצא מן העולם וחצי תאותו בידו אלא אם אית ליה מאה בעי דיעבדון תרתי מאה ומאן דאית ליה תרתי מאה בעי דיעבדון ארבעה לענות בו.
>
> *No person leaves the world with half of what he desires in his hand. If he has 100, he wants 200. If he has 200, he wants 400.* (Koheles Rabbah 3:13)

In other words, a person who has 200 lacks more than a person who has 100, because the person who has 200 is also desperately missing the next 200, whereas the person who only has 100 is only missing another 100. (To illustrate: The fellow who has a Ford only wants a Lexus, but the fellow who has a Lexus wants - who knows? A Lamborghini?)

People tend to think that Mesila is an organization that helps poor or struggling families.

But the ones who stand to gain most from Mesila are actually those who *do* have enough, and just need to manage what they have in such a way that they'll be able to make it.

Even those who have lots of income need Mesila - because unless you know how to control your spending, your spending will control you. And that's true no matter how much money you have.

Student Resource no. 5: **Financial Instability: No One is Immune**

REASON #2:

Life & finances have their ups and downs: גלגל החוזר

Even if you have enough - or more than enough - money right now, you never know what the future is going to bring. Developing healthy financial habits *now* can serve you well in the future no matter what your circumstances are.

The recent economic crisis highlights how people who were once affluent can be reduced to financial difficulties almost overnight.

REASON #3:

If you have it, you have to use it wisely.

Everything you have is a gift from Hashem to be used in the best way possible, to achieve a higher goal. That means that you may not squander what you've been given. In order to accomplish the most with your money, you need to know how to manage your money efficiently.

Student Resource no. 6: **Wallpapering Your House with Shas: The Chofetz Chaim's Advice for Maximizing the Use of Your Assets**

Unit 2

Budgeting

Goals:

- To understand what a budget is and why it's necessary to have one
- To examine the step-by-step process of building and following a budget
- To explain the concept of cash flow and learn how to build a cash flow plan
- To learn how to keep finances orderly by distinguishing between the various aspects of one's finances
- To understand basic banking and checking procedures

We all have limited money at our disposal, yet there are unlimited possibilities as to what we can do with that money. So the challenge is to use our money in the way that will bring us the maximum benefit and cause us the least financial stress. Budgeting is not about restrictions, it's about giving you control over your finances and freedom to use your money as you see fit. Your budget doesn't tell you how to spend your money – you tell your budget how you want to spend your money.

Note: *The Mesila Student Guide to Budgeting appears as its own section at the end of the book.*

1. What's a Budget?

Budgeting means managing any type of limited resource. In this case it's a plan for managing your money, based on your estimated income and expenses.

The idea of budgeting one's money makes many people tense, because they automatically associate "budget" with "I cannot afford what I want." A creative and effective way of introducing this topic is to discuss and/or have a class exercise in budgeting time or some other resource - i.e., "You have 3 hours available and you have the following tasks you'd like to accomplish. How will you budget your time? What will you give up? What is indispensable?" This exercise will lay the foundations for the principles of budgeting, which can then be easily transferred to financial budgeting.

2. Why Budget?

(see Part 4 - Mesila Guide to Budgeting, p. 4)

a. Control over your finances
b. Freedom to decide what you want to do with your money
c. Reduced financial stress

3. First Step: Prioritize

(see Part 4 - Mesila Guide to Budgeting, p. 5-7)

a. Our goal in budgeting is to allow you to have everything you need and some of what you want. That means that you have to know the difference between what you need and what you want. It also means that you have to make sure first that you have what you need, and only then see if you can have what you want.

   Note: This is a good place for class discussion about how to distinguish needs from wants, how it will differ in different societies, etc.

b. Needs before wants: Make sure you are aware of what your needs are so that you can fit them into your budget first, and only then see which of your wants can fit in.

c. Urgent vs. non-urgent: ***Discussion:*** what's the difference between urgent and important? When does the urgent override the important and vice versa?

d. Types of expenses:
   1) Fixed monthly expenses: mortgage or rent, insurance (life, health, home, auto, etc.), car payments, childcare, savings plans, domestic help, etc.
   2) Fluctuating monthly expenses: food, utilities (telephone, cellular phone, electricity, water, gas, etc.), gasoline, etc.
   3) Annual/Periodic expenses: summer camp, medical and dental costs, vacations and outings, home repairs

e. Tracking your expenses

   1) Why track? Knowing what you spend your money on and how much you spend will put you more in control of your money and help you make smarter spending decisions. Knowledge is power.

   2) How to track expenses: See addendum - The Mesila Guide to Budgeting

   3) Exercise: Track What You Spend! *(see Part 4 - Mesila Guide to Budgeting, p. 8)*
   For one week, track every single expense, even a can of soda, as well as every bit of income, including allowance, tutoring, babysitting. The goal is not yet to balance expenses and income, but to raise awareness.

4. Building a Family Budget

(see Part 4 - Mesila Guide to Budgeting, p. 9-16 & 37)

a. Monthly vs. Annual Budgeting

1) Some expenses occur every month, while others crop up once a year or periodically.
2) One of the most common mistakes people make in budgeting is calculating their monthly expenses but failing to take annual/periodic expenses into account. This is often the reason why people find themselves "not making it" when on paper their income seems adequate for their expenses.
3) Cash
4) Checks
5) Credit cards
6) Debit cards

b. Cash Flow Planning

1) Definition: Cash flow planning means ensuring that you have the money you need when you need it
2) Why is cash flow planning necessary? Income and expenses are not static - they fluctuate over the year. In order to ride out these peaks and troughs, you need to plan your budget to accommodate your cash flow needs.

c. Support material: Mesila budgeting forms

5. Maintaining Order: The Divide-and-Conquer Approach

(see Part 4 - Mesila Guide to Budgeting, p. 28-33)

a. Distinguishing between the many aspects of your finances is important because:

1) It helps you to gain an awareness of exactly what is happening with your money.
2) It puts you in control of your finances by enabling you to make informed decisions.

b. Differentiate between:

1) short-term and long-term expenses (e.g., weddings and retirement)
2) small purchases and major costs
3) predictable expenses and emergency/unforeseen expenses
4) personal expenses and business expenses

5) income and assets

6) ongoing expenses and debt

6. How Do I Know If My Budget Is Workable?

(see Part 4 - Mesila Guide to Budgeting, p. 36)

a. A good budget is one that does all of the following:

  1) Generously covers all essentials

  2) Leaves some room for non-essentials

  3) Makes provisions for unanticipated expenses

  4) Incorporates both short- and long-term savings

b. A budget has to be tested and adjusted, and updated regularly.

7. Long-term budget

(see Part 4 - Mesila Guide to Budgeting, p. 18-27)

a) Covers major expenses anticipated during the next few years

b) Includes both expected and unexpected expenses

c) Includes realistic savings and debt repayment strategies

PowerPoint presentation:

Basic banking and checking procedures

Unit 3

Leveraging Your Assets: Savings and Investments

Goals:

- To understand the importance of savings
- To examine different investment options
- To explain the risk/return equation
- To discover the power of compound interest

Money is a tool, a means to a higher purpose of good deeds and accomplishment. The money at our disposal can be used in a way that is beneficial or detrimental. Our challenge as Jews is to take the money that Hashem has given us and use it responsibly. Decisions about saving and investing money should be weighed carefully to ensure we treat money with proper seriousness.

A. Savings

Savings are a loan to yourself. It is no harder to put money away beforehand than to repay money afterward - you will need to strain yourself either way. The question is: Who are you paying? If you save, you end up paying yourself. (And you pay less money, because it's without interest, and also without embarrassment.) If you borrow, you are left with nothing at the end. And you have the stress of being beholden to someone and subject to his payment terms.

- **Torah view of savings**

  כל מי שיש לו פת בסלו ואומר מה אוכל למחר אינו אלא מקטני אמנה.

  One who has bread in his basket and says, "What will I eat tomorrow?" has a minimum of belief. (Sotah 48b)

- **Discussion:**

  How do we reconcile that concept with planning for the future?

Life Insurance

- Student Resource no. 7: **Life Insurance - To Buy or Not to Buy?**

- The Maharsha states in his *Chiddushei Aggados* (*Niddah* 65b) that a person should put aside money for his old age.
- In his Responsa *Shevet Halevi* (4:1), Harav Shmuel Wosner *shlita* writes, "It is obvious that [for] something that is the nature of the world, such as old age or marrying off children... it is a mitzvah to prepare in advance so that he will not become dependent on others."

B. Investments

1. Definition

Making your money work for you in order to make you more money.

2. Types of Investments

a) **Bank investments**

- The infinitesimal risks associated with bank investments make these the safest investments available. Because the risks are so low, the returns are also very low, occasionally lower than the rate of inflation. Bank investments are suitable for people with no risk tolerance, or for people who require immediate liquidity.
- Types of bank investments:

  (1) Savings account: an account in a bank on which interest is paid

  (2) Money market fund: a mutual fund which invests in short-term financial instruments, such as treasury bills and commercial paper

b) **Securities: Stocks & Bonds**

- **Stock:** the capital invested in a company or corporation through the buying of shares, each of which entitles the buyer to a share in the ownership and, usually, dividends, voting rights, etc.
- **Bond:** an interest-bearing certificate issued by a government or business, promising to pay the holder a specified sum on a specified date: it is a common means of raising capital funds
- **Mutual fund:** a fund consisting of a number of diversified securities that is owned jointly by those who have purchased shares in it as an investment
- **Hedge fund:** a partnership of investors who pool large sums for trading in securities, often taking large risks, as by buying with borrowed funds or selling short

c) **Real Estate**

Residential Real Estate

There are two types of potential earnings from residential real estate investments:

(a) Rent

(b) Capital gains (in the form of rising property value): The amount by which the selling price of an asset exceeds the purchase price; the gain is realized when the asset is sold.

(Definitions of above terms taken from Webster's New World Dictionary)

PowerPoint presentation:
Savings & Investments

D. Matching Your Savings Needs To Your Investment Strategies

1. The Risk/Return Equation

Investing, by definition, means risking capital for the sake of an anticipated future gain, or return. As a rule, return is directly proportional to risk – the greater the risk, the higher the potential return. The converse is true as well: the higher the potential return, the greater the risk.

- Student Resource no. 8: **Making Millions on Dinars**
  Young couples often have a nest egg that they are eager to invest. There are a lot of investments out there that promise sky-high returns – and carry with them sky-high risks. Currency speculation is one of them.
- Student Resource no. 9: **The Myth of Guaranteed Returns**
  If an investment is offering more interest than the bank offers, that means the bank is afraid to invest (otherwise they'd get financing from the bank). Is your risk appetite greater than the bank's?

2. Typical Fraudulent Investments

a) Pyramid Schemes

- A pyramid scheme is a dishonest and usually illegal business in which the money of later investors is used to pay the people who invested first.
- The fraudsters behind a pyramid scheme make their marketing scheme look real with many types of products or services. However, pyramid schemers simply use money coming in from new investors to pay off early stage investors.
- When they can't raise enough money from new investors to pay earlier ones, the pyramid scheme falls apart. As it comes crashing down, many people can lose lots of money.

b) Ponzi Schemes

- In both Ponzi and pyramid schemes, existing investors are paid by the money of new investors. But there is a big difference between a Ponzi and pyramid scheme.
- In a Ponzi scheme participants believe they are actually earning returns from their investment. In a pyramid scheme, participants are aware that they are earning money by finding new participants. They become part of the scheme. A Ponzi scheme is an investment trick.
- Ponzi scheme is named after Charles Ponzi. In the 1920s, Charles Ponzi tricked thousands of people into investing in a postage stamp scheme.At the time of his scheme, the annual interest rate for bank accounts was five percent. Ponzi promised investors a high return -- 50 percent -- in a very short amount of time. However, there were no investments. There were no honest returns. Ponzi used incoming funds from new investors to pay the returns to the earlier investors.
- A man named Bernie Madoff ran the largest and longest-running Ponzi scheme in the United States. It's approximated that Madoff made off with about $20 billion of investors' funds. One reason Madoff was able to fly under the radar for so long is because he was very well-known and trusted in the financial industry. He started his own investment firm in 1960 and helped start the Nasdaq stock market.But no matter how financially smart you are, a Ponzi scheme can only work if the clients keep their money in the scheme.In 2009, Madoff pleaded guilty to running a Ponzi scheme and stealing $17.5 billion from investors. He is serving a 150-year sentence in prison. But that is cold comfort to the thousands of investors, some of whom lost their entire life savings.

3. Short-Term vs. Long-Term Savings

- Short-term savings: The money you'll need for emergencies and for foreseeable large expenses.
- Long-term savings: The money you'll need for times of considerable financial strain, such as marrying off children and old age.
  - Student Resource no. 10: **Savings: The Long & Short of It**

  Your short-term savings goals and long-term savings goals require different strategies.

4. Liquidity

Being in cash or easily convertible to cash. This is an important consideration when saving or investing your money - how quickly and easily can it be converted to cash?

5. Tax Havens and Tax Shelters

Although tax haven and tax shelters go hand in hand to help high-net-worth individuals (HNWIs), and others, legally decrease their income tax burdens, there is an important difference between tax havens and tax shelters. Tax havens are locations around the globe known for having lax or nonexistent tax laws that allow individuals or companies to vastly reduce their tax liabilities by holding their assets offshore. Tax shelters are simply investment accounts, securities, investment and tax-planning strategies that minimize tax liability within your own country's tax system.

6. Types of Interest

- **Interest**
  a) Simple interest: interest calculated on principal alone, and not on principal plus interest (this is rarely relevant in investments or borrowing)
  b) Compound interest: interest calculated on the sum of the principal and the accrued interest (this is the type of interest typically earned on investments and paid on loans or credit cards)
  c) The power of compound interest: Over time, compound interest causes the principal to grow exponentially.

• Student Resource no. 11: **The Magic of Compound Interest**

The time value of money is the increase in an amount of money due to interest earned. Investing money rather than spending it today gives you a future amount worth more than you have now.

***Heter Iska*:** An agreement made between a borrower and a lender transforming a loan into an investment and turning borrower and lender into investor and manager who share in the possible profits or losses.

• See chapter 5, "Loans and Borrowing"

The Effect of Low Interest Rates

Interest rates were cut in the US to try and increase economic growth after the recession of 2008/09. Easy credit was seen as the culprit for the economic upheaval that led the fall of the stock market and the ensuing recession.

When the Federal Reserve (Fed) raises or lowers interest rates a chain reaction is set into motion. The Fed is the first domino and whatever they do — creates the chain reaction. If the fed raises interest rates, banks raise their prime rate, which in turn affects mortgage rates, car loans, business loans, and other consumer loans.

The period leading up to the recession of 2008/9 was characterized by high interest rates. Following the recession interest rates were brought down to almost unprecedented lows. Investors had to seriously change their strategy and mode of operation to stay relevant in the changed reality.

When consumers pay less in interest, this gives them more money to spend, which can create a ripple effect of increased spending throughout the economy.

When consumers pay less in interest, this gives them more money to spend, which can create a ripple effect of increased spending throughout the economy. Lower interest rates also make it cheaper to borrow. This tends to encourage spending and investment. This leads to higher demand for goods (aggregate demand) and economic growth. This increase often causes inflation.

What is the relationship between inflation and interest rates?

Inflation and interest rates are linked. Inflation refers to the rate at which prices for goods and services rises. In the United States, interest rates are determined by the Federal Reserve (the Fed). In general, as interest rates are lowered, more people are able to borrow more money. The result is that consumers have more money to spend, causing the economy to grow and inflation to increase. The opposite holds true for rising interest rates. As interest rates are increased, consumers tend to save as returns are higher. With less disposal income to spend as a result of the increase in savings, the economy slows and inflation decreases.

Investors and traders keep a close eye on interest rate decisions made by the Federal Open Market Committee FOMC. Certain markets may move in advance of the anticipated interest rate changes and in response to the actual announcements. For example, the U.S. dollar typically rallies* in response to an interest rate increase.

In theory, lower interest rates will:

- Reduce the incentive to save. Lower interest rates give a smaller return from saving. This lower incentive to save will encourage consumers to spend rather than hold onto money.
- Cheaper borrowing costs. Lower interest rates make the cost of borrowing cheaper. It will encourage consumers and firms to take out loans to finance greater spending and investment.
- Lower mortgage interest payments. A fall in interest rates will reduce the monthly cost of mortgage repayments. This will leave householders with more disposable income and should cause a rise in consumer spending.
- Rising asset prices. Lower interest rates make it more attractive to buy assets such as housing. This will cause a rise in house prices and therefore rise in wealth. Increased wealth will also encourage consumer spending as confidence will be higher.
- Depreciation in the exchange rate. When interest rates are reduced, it makes it relatively less attractive to save money. Therefore, there will be less demand for dollars causing it to fall in value. A fall in the exchange rate can make US exports more competitive and imports more expensive depending on levies and taxes.

A cut in interest rates will have a different impact on different groups within society.

- Lower interest rates are good news for borrowers, homeowners (mortgage holders). This group may spend more.
- Lower interest rates is bad news for savers. For example, retired people may live on their savings. If interest rates fall, they have lower disposable income and so will probably spend less.
- If a country has a high proportion of savers then lower interest rates will actually reduce the income of many people.

* A rally is a period of sustained increases in the prices of stocks, bonds or indexes. This type of price movement can happen during either a bull or a bear market, when it is known as either a bull market rally or a bear market rally respectively. However, a rally will generally follow a period of flat or declining prices.

Unit 4

Spending and Credit

Goals:

- To examine the various methods of payment and learn how to use each one optimally
- To examine the positive and negative aspects of consumerism
- To understand the importance of credit and how to build a good credit history
- To illustrate the advantages and pitfalls of credit cards

Spending often comes in two varieties – stinginess and extravagance, representing the two polar extremes of the spending spectrum. Our goal is to find a middle road that allows us to spend enough to meet our needs and obligations, but not so much that we squander money needlessly. Credit cards can be a very useful and convenient tool, when used correctly. The trouble is that many people misuse their credit cards by charging more than they can afford each month.

A. Payment Methods - Pros and Cons

- Student Resource no. 12: **Payment Methods chart**

B. Consumerism

1. Consumerism: Great for the Economy

a. Consumerism - definition: The theory that increasing consumption is economically beneficial

b. Increased consumption and spending leads to higher standard of living, improved quality of life and greater national wealth.

c. In other words: Shopping, buying, owning, acquiring are great for the economy, and therefore have been actively encouraged in the past century.

d. A healthy economy is dependent upon the movement of currency. When you buy groceries, the grocery owner can pay his tuition, and then the teachers and principals can buy food in the grocery. It's a cycle - money moves from hand to hand, benefiting everyone. When money doesn't move, and people don't spend, that results in a recession or depression.

e. This concept is supported in Torah sources as well:

ולמה נקרא שמם זוזין? שזזים מזה ונותנין לזה

Why is [money] called "zuzin"? Because it moves ["zaz"] from one and is given to another. (Bamidbar Rabbah 22:7)

f. Because spending has the power to create prosperity, people are encouraged to support local stores and businesses. This, too, is a Torah value:

נכנסו חכמי ישראל אצלו, אמרו לו: אדונינו המלך, עמך ישראל צריכין פרנסה.
אמר להם: לכו והתפרנסו זה מזה.

The Sages of Israel came to [Dovid Hamelech] and said to him, "Our master, the king, your nation Israel needs sustenance!" He said to them, "Go and earn a living from one another." (Berachos 3b)

g. Better than giving charity is giving people money in a dignified way, by employing them or patronizing their businesses.

2. Consumerism: Great for the Economy, But What About for Me?

a. Spending stimulates the economy, but at what cost to the individual?

b. The spending cycle - economically:

1. People are encouraged to spend money to stimulate the economy
2. People spend money, rather than conserve it
3. People start to need more because they have accustomed themselves to more
    - i. People run out of money and don't have savings to dip into
    - ii. People can't afford the things the things they are accustomed to
    - iii. People borrow money in order to pay for what they need and want
4. People fall into debt, which causes financial stress
5. Inability to maintain the standard of living that one has become accus-

tomed to results in stress and reduced quality of life

c. The impact of consumerism on people's values

1. People spend money, at the persuasion of advertising, rather than in response to real need.

2. The more they have, the more they need; consumerism is based on creating needs where none existed before

   Example: "The Lorax" by Dr. Seuss -

   Student Resource no. 13: **Dr. Seuss on Consumerism**

3. People become busier with spending

4. Advertising trains people to fill voids with spending

   i. People busy themselves with things instead of ideas

   ii. Relationships become shallow

   iii. Aspirations become materialistic and technical rather than value-based

   iv. People identify themselves with what they have and how they look rather than with their actions and character

   v. People fill voids in their life by acquisitions and shopping rather than introspection and growth

   vi. People are left feeling empty - and then they go spend more

3. Torah View of Consumerism

The Torah view of consumerism: Acquisition is not a value, but rather a tool toward reaching higher goals. Shopping and acquiring possessions is NOT a positive, constructive activity in and of itself, but rather a necessary chore.

4. Discussion: Shopping as Retail Therapy?

Note: Shopping is a favorite pastime for teens and young adults. Shopping malls do their part to transform the shopping trip into an "experience." Open the floor to discussion of the topic and guide the responses towards the desired conclusions.

People often go shopping as a form of leisure or to fill an emotional void. Is shopping a valid form of therapy or recreation? In what ways can this become a detrimental habit?

Discussion: Shopping as Retail therapy

By Carmen Shai (Global News)

Black Friday

They line up for hours outside in the cold, wading through swarms of people scouring the endless aisles of sales. These are daring Black Friday shoppers looking for a deal.

Black Friday is one of the biggest shopping days of the year - last year, consumers spent more than $11 billion, according to U.S. reports. But why do shoppers turn into spendthrifts, emptying their pockets and filling up their trunks during this 24-hour frenzy?

Dr. Laurence Ashworth calls Black Friday a "perfect storm" of a handful of psychological mechanisms.

"You have the possibility of getting a deal, which is very motivating already and on the flipside you have the strong possibility that you'll miss out on the deal. These two things working in concert causes exactly the kind of behavior that we see, the urgency, the rush and the desire to get ahead of other people," he told Global News.

"It's a manipulative plot that's not new in the shopping industry. If you want deals, you have to get them in within a certain period of time. It gets the mind going, 'I've got to get this deal' even if you don't want to buy it," Dr. Vera Tarman, a Toronto-based addictions expert, told Global News.

She says the adrenaline rush some consumers get from shopping and finding a bargain is akin to the thrill others get from gambling and even drugs.

It's an innate feeling - to want to indulge, to want to treat ourselves. Black Friday, with a week-long build-up of commercials and email reminders just builds up that tension.

Nicole McCance, a Toronto-based psychotherapist and author, says that lead up causes us to overspend. "You get really excited, you have to stand in line and it's one day only and you're shopping next to hundreds of people. By the time you go in, you're buzzing. It's perfect because people buy more when they're in that state of mind," McCance said.

The feel-good dopamine isn't a lingering feeling, though. By the time consumers are home, surrounded by their purchases, they aren't as satisfied with themselves, both Tarman and McCance say.

"They actually feel sick. They feel remorse because they're coming down from their high," Tarman explained.

Student Resource no. 14: **Am I a Shopaholic?**

So before you spend money, perhaps consider the following.

1. Think About the Work it Would Take

Suppose a meal at a restaurant costs $100. If you're wealthy, that might not seem like much. But how many hours of you babysitting/working/teaching will it take to pay for this? The decision to eat out probably doesn't seem as clear now, does it? Apply this logic to any purchase to assess if it is smart for you.

2. Consider the Cost Per Use

Consider how much each use of a given item will cost to determine whether it's worth the price. For example, if your neighbor offers to sell you his old car for $2,000, you may think that's cheaper than anything you'll find at a dealership, so it must be a great deal. But it isn't.

You soon discover that the car has numerous mechanical problems, has 250,000 miles on the odometer, and judging by the tire marks in your neighbor's driveway, was driven quite aggressively. You'll be lucky if you get more than a few months out of it.

That nearby car dealership, on the other hand, is selling a reliable model with far less wear and tear for a few thousand dollars more. This would likely be a much better deal, since you'd pay less per use, despite paying more up front.

3. Time is Money

Sometimes it's worth spending a little time to save a little money -- like cooking at home rather than paying twice as much to get a pre-made meal. But sometimes, working too hard to save a dollar wastes more time than it's really worth.

We've all heard stories about those extreme savers who spend an hour making their own laundry detergent, refill their condiment bottles with packets from fast food restaurants or spend an entire afternoon driving from store to store all across town for one or two items that are on sale.

When it comes to extremes like this, you need to ask yourself if your time investment is really worth the return you're getting. Spending hours of your life to save a few cents here or there is probably not worth it especially if you can make more money working.

4. Will the Item Last Longer

When it comes to items you use on a regular basis, sometimes it's worth shelling out a little more to buy a better-quality product that will last longer.

If you spend a lot of time on your feet, investing in a pair of high-quality shoes is much smarter than grabbing a cheap pair that will wear out in a matter of weeks.

If you live in an area that gets socked with snow in the winter, investing in a midrange snowblower makes more sense than buying the clearance model with the one-star reviews.

Think not just in terms of price, but also how much value you'll get for that price.

5. It Will Save you Money in the Future

Spending a little more each month to get better insurance coverage could save you hundreds, if not thousands, if you ever find yourself in a situation where you need to make a claim on that coverage.

Opting for regular car maintenance and preventative health care can save you from costly bills down the line if you neglect to keep things in good working order.

Fixing something right (and right away) rather than doing the bare minimum to keep it running (or, worse, paying a handyman with less-than-great credentials) is much smarter than doing shoddy work that will only result in a much worse (read: more expensive) repair bill later.

C. Understanding Credit

A. Credit - definition: The ability to pay later for goods or services

B. Credit history - definition: The record of one's past borrowing and repayment patterns, including information about late payments and bankruptcy

C. Why does credit history matter? Because when you apply for any sort of loan, mortgage, credit card, or financing, the lender will check your credit history to see whether you repaid previous commitments and whether you repaid them in a timely manner. If you have a bad credit history, or even if you don't have any credit history, you will have a very hard time convincing a bank or any company to lend you money or issue you a credit card.

D. Credit rating - definition: A score assigned to a person or business based on their credit history by which lenders can assess their likelihood to repay.

E. How do you establish a good credit history and credit rating?

A few tips:

1. By obtaining and using credit

   a. It's important to apply for a credit card and use it in order to start your credit history. 15% of your credit rating is determined by how long you've been borrowing.

   b. As you develop a good credit history, you can slowly apply for an increasingly higher credit limit so that you become a more "credit-worthy" consumer.

c. Although you need to use some of the credit extended to you in order to establish credit history, you should not use a high percentage of your credit limit, because that makes you a credit risk.

d. Too many inquiries into your credit history will damage your credit rating

Note: The purpose of using credit is not to borrow money to pay for purchases you can't afford; it's to establish yourself as a worthy borrower so that you can obtain credit in the future for big-ticket items such as mortgage or auto financing.

2. By making sure to pay your bills on time, whether it's your bill at the dentist or electric bill

3. By paying your credit card statement in full every month, on time, and never missing a minimum payment

D. Credit Cards: Pros and Cons

Student Resource no. 15: **Credit Card Scenarios**

A letter from Mesila to Mishpacha magazine:

To the Editor:

In response to your article entitled "The Newlywed Spending Bubble," Y.B. from Lakewood writes the following:

"For some of us, credit cards are a lifesaver. Shabbos comes every week, no matter what your financial status is, as do the Yamim Tovim, bar mitzvahs, weddings, and the like. Even if you don't buy the fanciest roast, you still need the basics, which can be burdensome for large families. And when your son's toe is at the end of his shoe or already popping through, you can't always wait until the funds are there."

As a Mesila counselor, I have to respectfully disagree with that statement. For a family that is struggling to pay for its basic needs, credit cards are not a lifesaver, but a dangerous trap. Putting purchases on a credit card is an easy way to pay for immediate needs, but it creates a much worse problem in its wake. If a family is already having a hard time making ends meet, paying an extra 15-30% in interest above and beyond the purchase price of everything on their credit card will surely make things harder.

Even if credit cards are a lifesaver in certain situations, a lifesaver is by definition something that should be necessary only in an emergency. Shabbos is not an emergency; nor are Yamim Tovim or simchas. And kids don't outgrow their shoes in a day or two. If a family is feeling the pinch from any of these normal, predictable expenses, credit cards are not the answer.

Y.B. goes on to write: "Some of us must have bitachon that, although we don't know how we will pay off our credit cards, if we are doing ratzon Hashem, we are confident that He will provide for us in some way or form."

This is a gross misapplication of the concept of bitachon, for bitachon does not justify acting in a way that is financially irresponsible. Charging things to your credit card and then waiting for money to miraculously appear is a highly dangerous habit, and one that the Ultimate Provider will not necessarily underwrite.

So what is a struggling family to do when there are bills that need to be paid, but no money to pay them with?

For one thing, they can seek creative, low-cost alternatives to ensure that the family is adequately fed and attired. They can also build a spending budget that maximizes every dollar and allows them to meet their basic needs while avoiding unnecessary expenditures. And a prime example of an unnecessary expenditure is money paid to the bank in the form of interest on credit card debt!

It is also critical for every family - even a family that is having a hard time making ends meet - to put aside cash on a regular basis. Even if all you can manage to put aside is $10 a week, the money will build up steadily, giving you your own little fund to turn to in a pinch - instead of having to look to greedy credit card companies for illusory salvation.

Aryeh Katz, Baltimore

Mesila's answer: In Eretz Yisrael, the big crisis is gemachim and overdraft, and the easy availability of loans, which causes people to borrow way more than they can afford to pay back. But make no mistake about it - the credit card crisis in the frum community in America is far worse, and much more insidious. How many people are walking around with a credit card debt of tens of thousands of dollars - and growing every day? How many of you know someone whose life has been ruined by credit cards? And how do you think it started? It never starts with $50,000, or even with $5,000. It starts with ONE purchase that you can't afford to pay for that creates your first small monthly balance. The first time you carry over a balance to the next month, what happens? NOTHING! The balance is only a bit bigger the next month. And once you have a small balance, what's so bad if that little balance becomes a bit bigger? It's a slippery slope...

We all know this. You've heard this before. So why are so many people falling into the same trap? Are you all going to walk out and throw out your credit cards, never to use a credit card again? No? Why not?

Obviously credit cards CAN be used, but only if they are used responsibly by people who NEVER, EVER pay late and don't charge things if they can't afford to pay their bills.

What does Mesila say about credit cards? We say: It's a tool that can be useful if used responsibly and dangerous if used irresponsibly. (Is a knife good or bad?)

Why do people buy things they can't afford? See chart on next page.

Discussion: Why do people buy (or charge) things that they can't afford (i.e., you don't have the money for RIGHT NOW)?

Pros and Cons of Credit Card Use

Advantages	Pitfalls
1. Convenient and available. 2. You can easily cancel the card if you lose it. In contrast, cash that is lost or stolen is usually gone forever. 3. You can use your credit card to pay for purchases by telephone or online, rather than mailing a check or paying by cash in person. 4. Most credit cards can be used anywhere in the world, regardless of the local currency, and you can order cards for all of your family members. 5. Depending on the card issuer's policy, purchases made using the card may be protected against theft, loss, or accidental damage that occurs within a certain period of time. 6. Credit card statements make it relatively straightforward to track your purchases on a monthly basis and keep a record of how your money is being spent. Cash, on the other hand, has no paper trail, and it is difficult to remember exactly where the money in your wallet went. 7. The possibility of earning rewards multiple ways by letting you choose between points, cash back, and airline miles. Many credit card companies also have a variety of retailers at which you can get discounts. 8. Depending on the type of card, you may have the benefit of car rental insurance, reimbursement for the cost of your flight should you cancel due to sickness or injury, lost luggage coverage, roadside assistance, extended warranty on a wide variety of purchases, price protection if the price of an item goes down shortly after you've purchased it and return guarantees.	a. Credit cards deceive people into thinking that they have money when they really do not. b. People spend more because it is convenient and because they do not feel the pain of parting with their money. c. Multiple credit cards can lead to chaos. d. Missing a minimum payment can lead interest rates to skyrocket. e. Carrying a balance from month to month (which over 60% of users do) f. Sky-high interest rates: The difference between a low interest rate and a high interest rate can be enormous. Someone with an $8,000 credit card balance who makes minimum monthly payments of 2.5% of the balance:

Let's examine what differences in credit card rates will mean long term.

Amount of Loan	What's the interest rate?	How long will it take to pay off?	How much interest will be paid in total?
$8,000	18%	30 years	$ 11,615.32
$8,000	12%	20 years, 1 month	$ 5,180.13
$8,000	9%	18 years, 2 months	$ 3,334.52
$8,000	5.9%	16 years, 1 month	$ 1,907.18

Choosing the Best Card

Plan wisely, particularly if you have multiple cards. You may choose to use one main card for the vast majority of your purchases but have a second emergency card in case you lose your wallet. To make the most of credit card rewards, plan these strategically: For some people, their primary card is their cash back card, but you may also have a second card so you can save up points towards a free vacation. A third card may be most advantageous for gas purchases. Do your homework to ensure you are getting the most out of each one, but most importantly, keep track of each card and its payment schedule.

Know What You're Really Getting by Paying Attention to the Details.

What may appear best on the surface might not actually be best. For example, the fine print of a credit card may say that you'll get "up to 1%" cash back, meaning that some rewards may actually give back less than 1%. Some cards like American Express will give you a $100 gift card for 1,000 points - a penny for a point, but not all companies will give such a good ratio. You may think that a credit card is giving 10% back on purchases, but the fine print might state that you can only get that kind of percentage on the first $200 in purchases or for the first six months. It may not be as good as it appears at first glance.

Some credit cards limit the categories that count for rewards (like hotels vs. restaurants vs. gas stations). For some cards, your ability to get cash back on gas may even depend on whether you buy inside from the clerk or at the pump. One card might give back 5% to 10% on gas, but only a 0.5% on everything else—that might not be as good as a card that gives a smaller percentage on gas, but 1% on everything else. Pay attention to these details before signing up. Specifics change all the time, so keep track of all the policy changes that may occur.

Most important tip of all: Pay your bill on time or none of this has value!

There really aren't going to be very many rewards if you don't pay your credit card in full monthly, because you will just negate your rewards with fees and interest.

- Student Resource no 16: **Climbing the Mountain of Credit Card Debt**

There's a tefillah we say practically every day, sometimes a few times a day. Do we mean it? ונא אל תצריכנו - let's do everything we can to truly merit parnassah in the most dignified way possible, מתחת ידך המלאה. Much of it is in our hands.

Supplementary material:

PowerPoint presentation:

The ABCs of Credit Card Finance

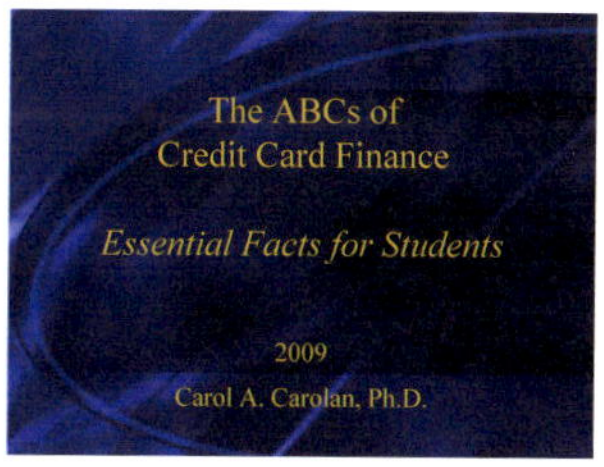

Unit 5

Loans & Borrowing

Goals:

- To differentiate between the various types of loans
- To introduce the benefits and costs of home ownership
- To discuss the positive and negative aspects of loans from religious and practical viewpoints
- To understand the psychological aspects of borrowing

Years ago, if someone did not have money to spend, he saved up until he had it. Today, it is hard to live with what we have because borrowing is so easy. Credit cards, payment plans, bank loans and gemachs are easily available. Buying on credit is also a form of borrowing. Of course it is a mitzvah to lend to others, but it is also a Torah obligation to pay back on time. A loan is not "easy money;" it is a responsibility.

They say it happened...

Jews and "choivos" have a long history. A Jew and a gentile each win a million dollars in a lottery.

The Jew asks the gentile, "What are you going to do with the money?"

"Well, first I'll buy my dream home, then I'll buy a yacht, and the rest I'll put into my retirement fund."

"And what are YOU going to do with the money?" the gentile asks the Jew.

"Well, I'll pay off my debts."

"And the rest?" the gentile asks.

"The rest of the choivos will have to wait," the Jew says.

Where did this Jew get a million dollars in debt? Who lent him the money?

Discussion: Open discussion of loans - good or bad? Steer discussion towards recognition that loans can be dangerous when not controlled but may be necessary at times. Important to benefit from loans with great caution.

A. Types of Loans

1. Bank loan
2. Line of credit
3. Business loan
4. Student loan
5. Gemach loans
6. Private loans
   a. From friends or family
   b. From finance companies or private commercial lenders
7. Store credit
8. Loan guarantees (ערבות)
9. Mortgages

- Student Resource no. 17: **Trading Securities**

Mortgages

2. Hidden benefits of home ownership
   a. Property values typically rise over time.
   b. Rents go up because of inflation; mortgages don't. That means that even if paying a mortgage is difficult at first, it usually becomes easier as time goes on.
   c. You have equity (value of the property minus the amount owed on it), which offers a measure of financial stability.
   d. Psychological comfort of owning your own home and feeling settled

3. Hidden costs of home ownership
   a. Property tax
   b. Utilities
   c. Maintenance (more cleaning, gardening, home upkeep, extermination, etc.)
   d. Transportation costs are higher when you live in the periphery
   e. Tuition goes up when you are a homeowner
   f. Homeowner's insurance

4. Home ownership scenarios:

Contrast the approaches taken by the two couples above. What are the long-term ramifications of each approach?

Couple #1	**Couple #2**
Shmuel and Suri Rosenblum have an $80,000 nest egg: $60,000 put away from wedding money and money that Suri has saving since high school, plus $20,000 that their parents gave them toward a house, which costs them $285,000. They take out a $205,000 mortgage, and they scrimp and save to meet their $1400 mortgage payments, which is slightly more than they can afford. To ensure that they can meet their payments, they cut a lot of corners: they don't take vacations, they manage with an old car, they don't buy takeout or extras in the supermarket, and they buy clothing only at end-of-season sales. Within five years, the value of their house climbs to $380,000.	Avi and Ayala Stern have $80,000 from an insurance settlement that Avi received after being in a car accident. They put the money into a savings account and dip into it as needed - for furniture, a car, little gifts for each other and for their friends, going out to eat. They are renting a house for $1400/month, which is slightly more than they can afford, but when the going gets tough, they always have their nest egg to fall back on. Within five years, the $80,000 is gone - and their rent has gone up to $1700.

- Student Resource no. 18: **Mortgage Payments & Interest**

B. Torah View of Loans

Torah commandment to lend money: אִם כֶּסֶף תַּלְוֶה אֶת עַמִּי - When you will lend my nation money (*Shemos* 22:24) - see Unit VI, charity section. But what about taking a loan? That's not a mitzvah. In fact, let's see what the Torah's view on taking loans is:

1. There's a mitzvah to lend money

Sefer Ahavas Chessed chap. 1

מצות עשה מן התורה להלוות לעניי אחינו, שנאמר (שמות כב, כד) אם כסף תלוה את עמי את העני עמך וגו'", ואיתא במכילתא דכל "אם" שבתורה רשות, ושלושה מהן חובה, וזה אחד מהן. וראיה ממה שאמר הכתוב "והעבט תעביטנו" - דרך ציווי. ומצוה זו גדולה יותר ממצות הצדקה, שאין העני בוש בדבר כל כך. גם שבזה תומך ידו ומחזיק אותו שלא יתמוטט לגמרי, ומקיים בזה מה שאמר הכתוב (ויקרא כה, לה): "וכי ימוך אחיך ומטה ידו

עמך, והחזקת בו וגו'", דהיינו שיחזיק בו עד שלא יפול ויצטרך לבריות. ומצוה גם כן להלוות לעשיר לפי שעה [היינו לזמן מועט] בשעה שאין המעות מצוי לו, דגמילות חסד נוהג בין לעניים בין לעשירים, אלא דהעני קודם לו בזה, ולכך פירט הכתוב לעני במצוה זו. ואי לא דהודיענו הכתוב, היה רצונו של אדם יותר להלוות לעשיר, מפני שגם הוא ישיג פעמים רבות טובות ממנו, ועוד שהעשיר בטוח אצלו יותר. ב) ודע עוד, דלאו דווקא הלוואת מעות, דהוא הדין דמצוה להשאיל לו כליו ושאר חפציו כיוצא בזה.

2. There's also a mitzvah to repay a loan

Sefer Ahavas Chessed chap. 24

הנה עד כה בארנו גודל המצוה של הלוואה, ועתה נבאר את גודל החיוב שמוטל על הלווה לפרוע חובו. אמרו חז"ל כתובות (פו.): פריעת חוב - מצוה היא. ולא יוכל להשתמט עצמו מזה, כמו שאינו יכול לפטור עצמו מסוכה ושופר ותפלין, עיין שם בגמרא. בוא וראה עד כמה גדול כוח החיוב הזה, שהרי אמרו חכמינו זכרונם לברכה בבא מציעא (קיג:): דמסדרין לבעל חוב [היינו מי שאינו משלם בעצמו, ובא המלוה לגבות בכח בית דין], ומניחין לו מזון שלושים יום, וכסות על שנים עשר חודש ולא יותר, וכלי אומנות שהוא מוכרח למלאכתו, וכל שאר מטלטליו וספריו וקרקעותיו מוכרין הכל בשביל בעל חוב, ואין מניחין אפילו למזונות אשתו ובניו, דכל מה שיש לו משועבד בשביל חובו.
והמונע את עצמו מלפרוע חובו כשיש לו, מפני אלמות שיש בו - הוא עובר על מה שכתוב בתורה (ויקרא יט, יג): "לא תעשוק את רעך וגו'". וכדאיתא בחושן משפט סימן שנ"ט סעיף ח': איזהו עושק? זה שבא ממון חברו לתוך ידו ברצון הבעלים, וכיון שתבעוהו כבש הממון בחזקה ולא החזירו, כגון שהיה לו ביד חברו הלוואה או שכירות והוא תובעו, ואינו יכול להוציא ממונו מפני שהוא אלם וקשה, עד כאן לשונו.
וגם אמרו חכמינו זכרונם לברכה (במדבר רבה פרשה יח, יב): ארבעה נקראו רשעים, ואחד מהם: הלווה ואינו משלם, שנאמר (תהלים לז, כא): "לוה רשע ולא ישלם". וכמה יש לו לאדם להתבייש מעצמו, כשיודע שהיכולת בידו לפרוע, והוא מונע עצמו מזה, ומביא על עצמו שם רשע. דהלא אם יקראהו חברו רשע, אפילו בינו לבין עצמו שלא הגיע לו על ידי זה שום בזיון, אף על פי כן יכעס עליו מאד עבור זה, וכל שכן בזה שגרם לעצמו שנקרא שמו רשע עבור זה, כמה מהכלימה והחרפה ישיגהו לבסוף לעתיד לבוא כשיתפרסם שמו זה לפני רבי רבבות מחנות קדושות, כמו שכתבו הספרים הקדושים, שכל עניניו של אדם נכרזין ונתפרסמין למעלה לפני כל. ואף שהוא מיפה עצמו לפני אנשי גילו, שאין לו אשם בזה - הלא לפני השם גלוי גודל עלוותו. וזהו כוונת חז"ל באבות (פרק ב' משנה י"ג): "ואל תהיה רשע בפני עצמך". [ובפרט אם הוא תלמיד חכם - עוונו גדול מאד ומאד, שמתחלל שם שמים על ידי זה, ועובר עוד מלבד כל אלו הנ"ל על לאו (ויקרא כב, לב) ד"לא תחללו את שם קדשי". וגדולה מזו אמרו ביומא (פו.): היכי דמי חילול השם? כגון דאקיף ולא יהיב דמי לאלתר, וכל שכן בזה שאינו משלם כלל]. ואיתא בחושן משפט סימן צ"ז סעיף ד': אסור ללווה לקחת הלוואה ולהוציאה שלא לצורך ולאבדה, עד שלא ימצא המלוה ממה לגבות

חובו, ואם עושה כן - נקרא "רשע" וכל שכן היכי שיש לו ואינו רוצה לשלם, כמה גדול עוונו עבור זה.

גם צריך לידע, שממון אחרים שנשאר ביד אדם בעוול, לבסוף לא יצליח, וכדכתיב (ירמיה יז, יא): "עושה עושר ולא במשפט בחצי ימיו יעזבנו" [ו"יעזבנו" קאי על שניהם, כי פעמים יעזוב העושר את האדם, ולפעמים להיפך], ויכלה גם את יתר הפליטה שיש לו בעצמו מכבר, וכדאיתא במסכת דרך ארץ זוטא פרק ג': אם נטלת את שאינו שלך - את שלך יטלו ממך [ראה לעיל פרק א' ד"ה כן ממש]. וענין השמירה מממון אחרים נכלל במה שאמר הכתוב (מיכה ו, ח): "הגיד לך אדם מה טוב ומה ה' דורש ממך, כי אם עשות משפט וגו'", כי כל זה הוא בכלל חוקי המשפט, להיות האדם זהיר שלא לעשות עוול לחבירו. ועיין לעיל בפרק א' שהארכתי בענין זה. והשומר עצמו להתנהג בדרך המשפט, הוא מהמקרבים ישועת השם על ישראל, וכדכתיב (ישעיה נו, א): "שמרו משפט ועשו צדקה, כי קרובה ישועתי לבוא וצדקתי להגלות". ועיין מה שכתבנו בקונטרס "שפת תמים" בפרק ג' וד' וה'.

C. Considerations When Taking Loans

It is a mitzvah to give a loan, and to repay a loan - but it is NOT a mitzvah to borrow. In fact, loans are inherently negative and problematic.

1. Hashkafah Considerations When Taking Loans

- **It is a blessing not to need loans:**

Devarim 28:12

יִפְתַּח ה' לְךָ אֶת אוֹצָרוֹ הַטּוֹב אֶת הַשָּׁמַיִם לָתֵת מְטַר אַרְצְךָ בְּעִתּוֹ וּלְבָרֵךְ אֵת כָּל מַעֲשֵׂה יָדֶךָ וְהִלְוִיתָ גּוֹיִם רַבִּים וְאַתָּה לֹא תִלְוֶה. (מהברכות בפרשת כי תבוא)

Hashem will open for you His treasure-house of goodness, the heavens, to give the rain of your land in its time and to bless all your handiwork and you will lend to many nations and you will not borrow.

- **Taking loans is a misfortune:**

Devarim 28:44

הוּא יַלְוְךָ וְאַתָּה לֹא תַלְוֶנּוּ (מהקללות בפרשת כי תבוא)

He will lend to you and you will not lend to him.

Urim V'Tumum 267

למה אין מברכין על מצות הלוואה? כיון שהוא קללה ופורעניות. דבברכה נאמר "ואתה לא תלווה" (דברים כח:יב) וכן "ואפס כי לא יהי' בך אביון" (שם טו:ד). ועוונותיו הטו את אלה, משום כך אין לברך עליו.

• Every time we recite *Birkas Hamazon*, we ask that we not be reduced to taking loans:

Birkas HaMazon

ונא אל תצריכנו ה' אלקינו לא לידי מתנת בשר ודם ולא לידי הלוואתם.

• Taking loans corrupts a person's soul:

Igros Chazon Ish 2:12

...לשלוח יד בהלוואות, המשחית את אצילות הנפש, וגורם בושה לעצמך ולאחרים.

• Loans that bear interest are even more problematic than non-interest bearing loans – even when the loan is halachically permitted, such as when there's a *Heter Iska* (see sample *heter iska* in resource 12):

Rashi Shemos 22:24

רבית שהוא כנשיכת נחש שנושך חבורה קטנה ברגלו ואינו מרגיש ופתאום הוא מבצבץ ונופח עד קדקדו, כך רבית אינו מרגיש ואינו ניכר עד שהרבית עולה ומחסרו ממון הרבה.

• A person who does not repay a loan can be considered a rasha, an evil person:

Pirkei Avos 2:9

אמר להם צאו וראו איזוהי דרך רעה שיתרחק ממנה האדם. רבי אליעזר אומר, עין רעה. רבי יהושע אומר, חבר רע. רבי יוסי אומר, שכן רע. רבי שמעון אומר, הלווה ואינו משלם. אחד הלווה מן האדם כלווה מן המקום ברוך הוא, שנאמר (תהלים לז) לוה רשע ולא ישלם, וצדיק חונן ונותן.

Bamidbar Rabba 18

שנו רבותינו **ארבעה נקראו רשעים**, הפושט ידו לחבירו להכותו אע"פ שלא הכהו נקרא רשע שנא' (שמות ב) ויאמר לרשע למה תכה רעך, הכית לא נאמר אלא תכה, **והלווה ואינו משלם** שנא' (תהלים לז) לוה רשע ולא ישלם וצדיק חונן ונותן, ומי שיש בו עזות פנים ואינו מתבייש לפני מי שגדול הימנו שנא' (משלי כא) העז איש רשע בפניו וישר הוא יבין דרכו, ומי שהוא בעל מחלוקת שנאמר סורו נא מעל אהלי האנשים הרשעים האלה.

2. Halachah Considerations When Taking Loans

Loans are not just hashkafically problematic, they may also be halachically forbidden at times (aside from the obvious halachic prohibition of interest):

1) It is forbidden to squander borrowed money to the extent that the borrower is subsequently unable to repay:

Shulchan Aruch Choshen Mishpat 97:4

אסור ללוה לקחת הלואה ולהוציאה שלא לצורך ולאבדה עד שלא ימצא המלוה ממה לגבות חובו ואם עושה כן נקרא רשע וכשהמלוה מכיר את הלוה שהוא בעל מדה זו מוטב שלא להלוותו ממה שילווהו ויצטרך לנגשו אחר כך ויעבור בכל פעם משום לא תהיה לו כנושה:

2) According to Rabbeinu Yonah, one may not take a loan if he does not know how he will pay it back - even if he is desperate for the money.

Rabbeinu Yonah Avos 2:9

ואם לא יכיר בשלו אם יהיה בידו יכולת לא ילווה עתה משום דוחק שיהיה לו וידחוק השעה גם אם הוא צריך הלוואה הרבה מאד... כיון שלווה ואינו משלם רשע הוא ואע"פ שאין לו, כי מתחילה היה לו לעיין במה יפרעהו, אבל הצדיק חונן מה שיש לו ליתן ולפרוע בהן נותנו, על כל פנים הוא נזהר מתחילה במה יוכל לפרוע...

3) In source (1) above, the *Shulchan Aruch* says that it is also forbidden to **lend** money to someone who will squander the loan and be unable to repay.

Note: See Shulchan Aruch and commentaries for further discussion of this complex halachic topic, see page 49.

4) **Discussion: Anticipating Consequences** – "הרואה את הנולד"

Pirkei Avos 2:9

אָמַר לָהֶם, צְאוּ וּרְאוּ אֵיזוֹהִי דֶרֶךְ יְשָׁרָה שֶׁיִּדְבַּק בָּהּ הָאָדָם. רַבִּי אֱלִיעֶזֶר אוֹמֵר, עַיִן טוֹבָה. רַבִּי יְהוֹשֻׁעַ אוֹמֵר, חָבֵר טוֹב. רַבִּי יוֹסֵי אוֹמֵר, שָׁכֵן טוֹב. רַבִּי שִׁמְעוֹן אוֹמֵר, הָרוֹאֶה אֶת הַנּוֹלָד. רַבִּי אֶלְעָזָר אוֹמֵר, לֵב טוֹב. אָמַר לָהֶם, רוֹאֶה אֲנִי אֶת דִּבְרֵי אֶלְעָזָר בֶּן עֲרָךְ מִדִּבְרֵיכֶם, שֶׁבִּכְלַל דְּבָרָיו דִּבְרֵיכֶם. אָמַר לָהֶם צְאוּ וּרְאוּ אֵיזוֹהִי דֶרֶךְ רָעָה שֶׁיִּתְרַחֵק מִמֶּנָּה הָאָדָם. רַבִּי אֱלִיעֶזֶר אוֹמֵר, עַיִן רָעָה. רַבִּי יְהוֹשֻׁעַ אוֹמֵר, חָבֵר רָע. רַבִּי יוֹסֵי אוֹמֵר, שָׁכֵן רָע. רַבִּי שִׁמְעוֹן אוֹמֵר, הַלֹּוֶה וְאֵינוֹ מְשַׁלֵּם. אֶחָד הַלֹּוֶה מִן הָאָדָם, כְּלֹוֶה מִן הַמָּקוֹם בָּרוּךְ הוּא, שֶׁנֶּאֱמַר (תהלים לז) לֹוֶה רָשָׁע וְלֹא יְשַׁלֵּם, וְצַדִּיק חוֹנֵן וְנוֹתֵן. רַבִּי אֶלְעָזָר אוֹמֵר, לֵב רָע. אָמַר לָהֶם, רוֹאֶה אֲנִי אֶת דִּבְרֵי אֶלְעָזָר בֶּן עֲרָךְ מִדִּבְרֵיכֶם, שֶׁבִּכְלַל דְּבָרָיו דִּבְרֵיכֶם:

We see from here that the ability to anticipate consequences (רואה את הנולד) is one of the five positive attributes that a person can possess. The corresponding negative attribute is borrowing without repaying (הלוה ואינו משלם) - one of the "top 5" things to avoid.

Question: Why is רואה את הנולד the opposite of הלוה ואינו משלם?

3. Practical Considerations When Taking Loans

a. DEBT CAN RUIN YOUR LIFE: The root of so many problems - shalom bayis, *chinuch*, health (physical, mental, emotional) - is financial pressure, which is created in large part by debt. When you owe money, you are a slave:

Mishlei 22:7

וְעֶבֶד לֹוֶה לְאִישׁ מַלְוֶה.

b. Headaches: Every loan involves time, energy, hassle, stress and embarrassment.

c. Debt juggling: When people borrow to repay old loans and end up desperately trying to juggle all their debts. This is a recipe for misery, not to mention financial disaster.

- Student Resource no. 19: **Sample Heter Iska Form for Business Loans**

D. Positive Loans vs. Negative Loans

1. Positive loans

a. Definition: A loan that yields returns in the long run

b. Examples:

1. Mortgage (you are left with a house after you pay the mortgage)
2. A business or investment loan (assuming the enterprise is a solid one, you should earn greater returns than the money you borrowed)
3. Using a credit card to establish a good credit history and credit rating

2. Negative loans

a. Definition: A loan that gets consumed with nothing left to show for it

b. Examples:

1. A debt to the grocery (by the time you pay your bill, you've already eaten all the food you bought - and what about next month?)
2. Borrowing money from a friend to tide you over until your parents give you money (by the time the money comes, you have to give most of it to your friend, and then you're in a pinch once again)

3. Borrowing money for something you can do without
4. Installment plans for items that you'll be paying for long after the item is gone

3. **The worst type of loan: Borrowing to cover ongoing expenses**
   a. Ongoing expenses MUST be covered by steady income. Otherwise, you will eat yourself out of house and home - literally.
   b. If you don't have enough money: Three possible solutions
      1. Increase your income
      2. Reduce your expenses
      3. Take financial support, government aid or charity
      4. There is no other solution - borrowing is NOT an option if you can't afford to pay it back!

E. Psychological Aspects of Borrowing

1. Why do people buy (or charge) things that they can't afford?

2. ***Discussion*** – possible reasons:
   a. "Everyone else has it"
   b. "It's such an insignificant amount of money"
      (introduce idea of פרוטה פרוטה מצטרפת - every penny adds up)
   c. "It's a great deal"
   d. "I really need it"
   e. "I have *bitachon* that things will work out and I'll be able to pay"
   e. "It's worth it" (perhaps the most common teenage response)

3. Why is debt more of a problem today than it was in the past? Do people have less today?
   a. Availability of credit
   b. High cost of basic living (a car, air conditioning, summer camp, etc. can be considered basic needs)
   c. Money is virtual - you don't feel it leaving your pocket, it's just a bunch of numbers on a screen

UNIT 5:
LOANS
AND
BORROWING

שלמה | השמטות מחלק ראשון | חכמת

[illegible]

עינים | חושן משפט צז הלכות גביית מלוה | מאירת | באר הגולה

הלכות גביית מלוה

צז להלוות לעני ושלא לנגשו ושלא לחבול כלי אוכל נפש ואלמנה והשבת העבוט ודין הסידור וכו ל סעיפים :

א [ס](א) א מצות עשה ג להלוות לעניי ישראל ב והוא מצוה גדולה [א] ג יותר מהצדקה י וקרובו עני קודם לעניים אחרים ועניי עירו קודמים לעניי עיר אחרת ס [ג] ואפילו עשיר שצריך להלוות מצוה להלוותו לפי שעה [ג] ולההנותו אף בדברים [ד] ולייעצו עצה ההוגנת לו :

ב [ס] ג ו אסור לנגוש את הלוה לפרוע כשיודע שאין לו ו ואפי' להראות לו אסור מפני שהוא נכלם בראותו למלוה ואין ידו משגת לפרוע :

ג [ו] ד ס אסור ללוה לכבוש ממון חבירו ולומר לו לך ושוב ומחר אתן ויש אתו :

ד ס אסור ללוה לקחת הלואה ה ולהוציאה שלא [ב] לצורך ולאבדה עד שלא ימצא המלוה ממה לגבות חובו ואם עושה כן י נקרא רשע [ז] וכשהמלוה מכיר את הלוה שהוא בעל מדה זו מוטב שלא ללותו ממה שילוהו ויצטרך לנגשו אח"כ ויעבור בכל פעם משום לא תהיה לו כנושה :

ה [ס] ג אם בא המלוה לב"ד למשכן ללוה או ליפרע ממנו יש לב"ד לעשות לו דין ו ולא יאמרו פלוני עני ואין לו ופלוני עשיר ואין צריך לו אלא אין מרחמים בדין :

ו ג אם בא למשכנו [ס] שלא בשעת הלואתו ז ב) א] לא ימשכננו הוא בעצמו שאם משכנו הוא [ג] בעצמו (ס) עובר בלאו (וע"ל ס' ד') אלא ב"ד ישלחו לו שלוחם ס ואף שלוחם לא יכנס לביתו למשכנו: הגה [י] ואפי' הם

[illegible]

באר הגולה | ביאור הגר"א | טורי זהב

[illegible]

באר הגולה | הטור

[illegible]

נתיבות המשפט | באר היטב

[illegible]

קצות | החושן

[illegible]

Unit 6

Charity, Integrity & Bitachon

Goals:

- To appreciate the significance of giving charity and loans to the needy
- To establish priorities in the giving of charity
- To appreciate the value of financial independence and being a "giver"
- To examine the concept of integrity in light of current realities
- To understand that financial responsibility is not a lack of *bitachon*

Sharing one's resources with others is not merely meritorious – it is an absolute obligation. In fact, the reason that some people have more and some people have less is because Hashem expects people to take responsibility for the poor and indigent and ensure that their needs are met as well.

A. Charity & Philanthropy: An Ethical Imperative

1. Charity is a Torah commandment emphasized repeatedly in Tanach.

כִּי יִהְיֶה בְךָ אֶבְיוֹן מֵאַחַד אַחֶיךָ בְּאַחַד שְׁעָרֶיךָ בְּאַרְצְךָ אֲשֶׁר ה' אֱלֹקֶיךָ נֹתֵן לָךְ לֹא תְאַמֵּץ אֶת לְבָבְךָ וְלֹא תִקְפֹּץ אֶת יָדְךָ מֵאָחִיךָ הָאֶבְיוֹן. כִּי פָתֹחַ תִּפְתַּח אֶת יָדְךָ לוֹ וְהַעֲבֵט תַּעֲבִיטֶנּוּ דֵּי מַחְסֹרוֹ אֲשֶׁר יֶחְסַר לוֹ... כִּי לֹא יֶחְדַּל אֶבְיוֹן מִקֶּרֶב הָאָרֶץ עַל כֵּן אָנֹכִי מְצַוְּךָ לֵאמֹר פָּתֹחַ תִּפְתַּח אֶת יָדְךָ לְאָחִיךָ לַעֲנִיֶּךָ וּלְאֶבְיֹנְךָ בְּאַרְצֶךָ:

If there will be among you a pauper from one of your brothers in one of your gates in your land that Hashem your God is giving you, you shall not harden your hard and you shall not close your hand from your impoverished brother. Rather, you shall surely open your hand to him and you shall lend him what he requires, whatever is lacking to him... For there will not cease to be a pauper in the midst of the land. Therefore I am commanding you saying, You shall surely open your hand to your brother to your poor and to your impoverished in your land. (Devarim 15)

2. Hashem provides for everyone, but the distribution is unequal - some people have more than they need while some have less. Why? Because He wants to give His people the merit of giving to others (*Sefer HaChinuch* 66).

שרצה הקֵל להיות ברואיו מלומדים ומורגלים במדת החסד והרחמים, כי היא מדה משובחת... ואם לאו מצד שורש זה הלא הוא ברוך הוא יספיק לעני די מחסורו זולתנו, אלא שהיה מחסדו ברוך הוא שנעשינו שלוחים לו לזכותנו.

Hashem wished to accustom humanity in the qualities of kindness and compassion, for those are exemplary qualities...If not for this underlying consideration, Hashem would provide for the pauper without us. But in His kindness, He made us His emissaries, in order for us to accrue merit.

3. Sharing one's resources with others is not merely meritorious - it is an absolute obligation. In fact, the reason that some people have more and some people have less is because Hashem expects people to take responsibility for the poor and indigent and ensure that their needs are met as well.

Ohr Hachaim on the verse אִם כֶּסֶף תַּלְוֶה אֶת עַמִּי - *When you will lend money to my people* (*Shemos* 22:24):

אם כסף תלוה את עמי, פירוש אם ראית שהיה לך כסף יותר על מה שאתה צריך לעצמך, שאתה מלוה לעמי, תדע לך שאין זה חלק המגיעך, אלא חלק אחרים שהוא העני עמך, ובזה רמז כי צריך לפתוח לו משלו ואולי כי רמז לו גם כן שלא יתנשא ויתגדל על העני, בראותו כי הוא הנותן לו, והוא אומרו לא תהיה לו כנושה, לשון נשיאות ומעלה, כי משלו הוא נותן לו.

The verse "When you will lend money to my people" means: If you see that you have more money than you require for yourself, and that you are able to lend to others, you should know that this is not your portion to which you are entitled, but rather the portion of others - namely, the pauper among you. With this, the Torah insinuates that a person must open to the pauper of his [the pauper's] own resources, and perhaps it is also intimating that he should not act condescendingly or arrogantly toward the pauper when he sees that he is the one giving to the pauper. That is the meaning of the verse, You shall not be as a creditor (nosheh) to him, nosheh being related to the word for haughtiness (nesius), for he is giving the pauper what rightfully belongs to him (the pauper).

4. When carrying out your responsibility to provide for others in need, realize that they are doing you a bigger favor than you are doing for them. For you are providing them with mere money or material assistance, while they are providing you with eternal merit. (*Vayikra Raba* 34:8)

> יותר ממה שבעל הבית עושה עם העני, העני עושה עם בעל הבית שכן רות אומרת לנעמי (רות ב) שם האיש אשר עשיתי עמו היום בועז אשר עשה עמי אין כתיב כאן אלא אשר עשיתי עמו.
>
> *More than the householder does for the pauper, the pauper does for the householder, as Rus said to Naomi, "The name of the man for whom I did today is Boaz." The verse does not say "who did for me" but rather "for whom I did."*

[In other words, Rus was implying that she did something for Boaz, though it would seem that he had given to her.]

B. *Maaser* and *Chomesh*: A Tenth and a Fifth

***Maaser*: A tenth**

1. From the time of Avraham, Yitzchak, and Yaakov, Jews have traditionally tithed their produce and income.
2. The minimum tithe is 1/10; the maximum is 1/5.
3. *Maseches Kesuvos* 50:

> המבזבז אל יבזבז יותר מחומש שמא יצטרך לבריות.
>
> *One who dispenses [charity] should not dispense more than a fifth [of his money], lest he become dependent on others.*

4. Exceptions to this 1/5 limitation (Source – *Ahavas Chessed* 20):
   (a) A person on his deathbed (there's no danger that he'll become dependent on society)
   (b) A very wealthy person
   (c) When hungry and indigent people approach the donor for help he has to feed and clothe them

(d) When the recipient's life is in danger

(e) For the support of Torah study

5. Possible uses for maaser money

(1) Some say it must be used for charity

(2) Others say it may be used for other mitzvos as well; ask a rabbi

C. The Mitzvah of Lending

מצות עשה מן התורה להלוות לעניי אחינו, שנאמר (שמות כב, כד) אם כסף תלוה את עמי את העני עמך גו'. ואיתא במכילתא דכל "אם" שבתורה רשות, ושלושה מהן חובה, וזה אחד מהן. וראיה ממה שאמר הכתוב "והעבט תעביטנו" דרך ציווי. ומצוה זו גדולה יותר ממצות הצדקה, שאין העני בוש בדבר כל כך. גם שבזה תומך ידו ומחזיק אותו שלא יתמוטט לגמרי, ומקיים בזה מה שאמר הכתוב (ויקרא כה, לה) וכי ימוך אחיך ומטה ידו עמך, והחזקת בו וגו' דהיינו שיחזיק בו עד שלא יפול ויצטרך לבריות. ומצוה גם כן להלוות לעשיר לפי שעה [היינו לזמן מועט] בשעה שאין המעות מצוי לו, דגמילות חסד נוהג בין לעניים בין לעשירים. אלא דהעני קודם לו בזה, ולכך פירט הכתוב לעני במצוה זו. ואי לא דהודיענו הכתוב, היה רצונו של אדם יותר להלוות לעשיר, מפני שגם הוא ישיג פעמים רבות טובות ממנו, ועוד שהעשיר בטוח אצלו יותר. ודע עוד, דלאו דווקא הלוואת מעות, דהוא הדין דמצוה להשאיל לו כליו ושאר חפציו כיוצא בזה.

It is a positive commandment from the Torah to lend to our impoverished brethren, as the verse states (Shemos 22:24), "When (im) you will lend money to my nation, to the pauper among you...." It is brought in the Mechilta that all instances of the word "im" in the Torah relate to optional actions, but three are obligations, and this is one of them. The proof to this is the Torah's statement "You shall surely lend to him," which is a direct commandment. This mitzvah is even greater than the mitzvah of charity, for the pauper is not as ashamed [when receiving a loan, as opposed to charity]. In lending a pauper money, one also supports his hand and strengthens him so that he should not collapse entirely, in fulfillment of the verse (Vayikra 25:35), "If your brother becomes impoverished and his hand falters near you, you shall strengthen him..." meaning that he should strengthen him to the point that he will not collapse and become dependent on others. It is also a mitzvah to lend to a wealthy person temporarily, at a time when he does not have money available, for the mitzvah of chessed applies to poor and rich alike, except that the pauper takes precedence over the wealthy person; that is why the verse specified the pauper in this commandment. Had the Torah not told us this, a person would have preferred to lend to the wealthy person, because he himself can often receive benefit from him, and also because he is more confident in the wealthy person. Furthermore, the mitzvah is not limited to lending money, for the halachah is that it is a mitzvah to lend a person his utensils and other objects and the like.

D. The Torah View on Financial Dependence

1. *Birkas Hamazon*:

ונא אל תצריכנו ה' אלקינו לא לידי מתנת בשר ודם ולא לידי הלוואתם.

Please do not make us needy of the gifts of human hands nor of their loans.

2. *Maseches Beitza* 32:

כל המצפה על שלחן אחרים עולם חשך בעדו... רב חסדא אמר אף חייו אינם חיים.

One who depends on others for sustenance, the world is dark for him... Rav Chisda says: In addition, his life is not a life.

a. *Chasam Sofer*:

והוסיף רב חסדא גם חייו בעה"ב אינם חיים כי כיון שלא זכה ליהנות מיגיע כפו דכתיב גביה אשריך בעה"ז וטוב לך לעה"ב וזה הוא ההיפך משניהם. אבל ת"ח איננו בגדר מצפה על שולחן אחרים, אלא בגדר ועמדו אחרים ורעו צאנכם, וק"ל:

b. Explanation of Chasam Sofer: What Rav Chisda is adding with his statement that "His life is not a life" is that his life *in the next world* is not a life, because he did not benefit from his own efforts, as the Talmud teaches that one who benefits from his own efforts is fortunate in both this world and the next world. However, a *talmid chacham* is not considered one who depends on others for sustenance; rather, because he is engaged in Torah study, he deserves to be freed from mundane matters (see *Berachos* 35b).

3. Jewish law mandates that a person go to great lengths to avoid being financially dependent (*Tur Yoreh Deah* 255:1-2).

> לעולם ירחיק אדם עצמו מהצדקה ויגלגל עצמו בצער שלא יצטרך לבריות וכן צוו חכמים עשה שבתך חול ואל תצטרך לבריות.
>
> *A person should always distance himself from charity and subject himself to affliction rather than being dependent on others, as the Sages instructed, "Make your Shabbos a weekday rather than be dependent on others."*

- Student Resource no. 20: **Taking Charity on a One-Time Basis**

Discussion: The concept of being a "giver" or a "taker" extends beyond charitable handouts. How else does this concept apply?

E. Priorities in Charity

1. **Yourself**
   a. חייך קודמים - Your life comes first (*Bava Metzia* 62a)
   b. פרנסת עצמו קודמת לכל אדם - Providing for oneself takes precedence over anyone else (*Rema, Yoreh Deah* 251:3)
   c. "Put on your own oxygen mask before assisting other passengers"
   d. Clearly, this applies to one's basic needs, not to extravagances.

2. **Your family: Charity begins at home**
   a. וּמִבְּשָׂרְךָ לֹא תִתְעַלָּם - And to your own flesh, you shall not be oblivious (*Yeshayah* 58:7)
   b. עניי ביתו קודמין לעניי עירו - The poor of one's household [i.e., one's family]

take precedence over the poor of one's city (*Shulchan Aruch Yoreh Deah* 251:3)

3. **Torah scholars** (enabling their Torah study).

מהנכון שיהדר לכתחילה לחלקם לעמלי תורה למען יחזקו בעבודת ה' כי משמע במדרש דעיקר המעשר נתקן בשביל להחזיק לעמלי תורה.

It is proper, most ideally, to distribute charity to those who study Torah, in order that they be strengthened in their Divine service, for it is understood from the Midrash that the requirement of maaser was instituted primarily in order to support those who study Torah.

4. **Other paupers**

Examples of other categories of precedence in giving charity:
(Note: This list is not exhaustive.)

a. The needy of one's city and the needy of the Land of Israel come before other needy individuals

b. A Kohen or Levi comes before a Yisrael

c. Parents come before other relatives (including adult children)

d. Food over clothing

e. Needy woman over needy man

See *Yoreh Deah* 251 for more details.

F. Integrity

1. Chazal tell us that the majority of people are tainted by theft (*Bava Basra* 165:a):

אמר רב יהודה אמר רב, רוב בגזל.

Rav Yehudah said in the name of Rav: Most [people are guilty] of theft.

2. A person never profits from lack of integrity (*sefer Chassidim*, 1075-1076).

המלוה בריבית, ממונו יכלה, או הגוזז מעות וכן העושה עולה במשקל במדה ובמשורה ובסחורות ובכל מיני עולה, לבסוף ירדו מנכסיהם, ובניהם

יתפרדו זה מזה בארץ נכריה, ונצרכים לבריות. וגם כל שיהיו חביריהם וכל הנלוה אליהם יכלה ממונם, וכל שיהיה מסייע להם.

One who lends with interest, his money will be wiped out; as well as one who embezzles money, or cheats in weights, measures, merchandise or any other fraud. Eventually, they will lose their money, and their children will be estranged from one another in a foreign land and be dependent on others. In addition, all those who befriend these [unscrupulous] people and all those who are attached to them, their money will be wiped out. The same will happen to alll those who facilitate them.

3) **Discussion topics:**

  i) How do you define integrity? Why do people generally view themselves as honest, when Chazal say that the majority of people have failings in this area?

  ii) Ways that people might steal without even realizing

    (1) Borrowing without permission

    (2) Copying music or written materials

    (3) Taking unfair advantage of store return policies

    (4) Taking hotel property or food

    (5) Withholding or delaying payment for goods or services

    (6) Etc.

G. Bitachon

Responsibly managing one's finances does not constitute lack of bitachon, but rather necessary *hishtadlus*.

- Student Resource no. 21: **Bitachon & Budgeting**

Note: These topics are complex, and the actual halachah often depends on the circumstances.

Part 2:

Student Resources

STUDENT RESOURCE 1

MESILA'S GUIDELINES FOR FINANCIAL STABILITY

Charity & Financial Independence

1 Bailing people out of their financial predicaments almost guarantees that they will repeat their mistakes.

2 Although handouts, including government assistance, are necessary at times – to make sure that a person does not go hungry, for instance – it must be remembered that any time a person gets something for nothing it increases dependence and decreases motivation.

3 Accepting charity is a last resort and should be avoided if at all possible.

4 Taking charity is preferable to taking a loan without having a source from which to repay.

5 Financial independence is measured by degrees, and is not an all-or-nothing proposition. Every bit of improvement is significant.

Hishtadlus (Effort)

6 Success in any financial endeavor depends on *siyatta dishmaya*. But the fact that the outcome is in Hashem's hands does not absolve people of the obligation to invest the necessary effort into any enterprise they embark on.

7 From the time of Adam HaRishon, *parnassah* was meant to be difficult, and the fact that someone experiences difficulties does not mean he is doing anything wrong.

8 A person should always strive to improve his financial situation.

9 Every person has been endowed by Hashem with talents, skills or knowledge that can be used to generate income.

Risk

10 For every person, there is an appropriate level of financial risk, and it is important for every person to take certain risks.

11 There is no such thing as a no-risk venture.

Change

12 Lasting economic change happens naturally, from the ground up. It cannot be imposed on any person or community.

13 Sustainable long-term improvement in a person's financial situation is usually possible only if the person is actively involved in the change.

14 A person who does not want help cannot be helped. And no one can be forced to change his financial attitudes or habits.

15 As a means of achieving financial stability, increasing income is preferable to reducing expenditures, since reducing expenditures is liable to cause stress and friction in the home, and reductions are not always sustainable long-term.

16 Extreme financial measures do not last.

Counseling

17 A person should never be embarrassed to seek financial guidance.

18 When people are in the midst of difficult financial situations, they are often powerless to extricate themselves from their predicaments. A fresh pair of eyes is therefore immeasurably helpful.

Money & Possessions

19 Money is a means, not an end, and its importance must be kept in the correct proportion.

20 Money alone does not usually solve money problems.

21 There is no such thing as easy money.

22 No matter how high a standard of living a person maintains, there should always be things that he refuses himself and his children.

23 In any financial situation a person could possibly be in, there will be things that he will not be able to have.

Human Nature

24 People do not work with precise financial calculations; they work with estimates. And when estimating, the natural tendency is to err on the side that is more convenient.

25 Financial limitations create motivation. If a person feels limited to spending only what he has, he will be motivated to earn money so that he will have what to spend. But if a person gets used to borrowing money, his sense of financial limitation broadens to include all of the money he can potentially borrow, which decreases his motivation to earn money.

26 Financial structure creates freedom. In homes that run with a budget, money is generally less of an issue than in homes where spending limits are only loosely defined.

27 Expenses rise to meet income, because when funds are available, they find a destination. And when people's income rises, their needs rise, too – but their needs usually rise more than their income.

28 People prefer not to confront unpleasant realities.

29 The tendency is that people seek financial solutions outside of themselves, even though most viable solutions are found within their own resources.

Solutions to Financial Problems

30 Solutions to financial problems must be comprehensive, if they are to last. If even one contributing factor is not dealt with as part of the solution, the problem will likely fester and recur.

31 Flawed financial attitudes and habits are often a factor – and often the main factor – in financial difficulties, so the quest for comprehensive, lasting solutions must involve replacing these attitudes and habits with healthy ones.

32 Every person can be helped, and every financial situation can be improved, at least to some extent.

33 There are no instant or easy solutions to complex financial challenges.

34 Solutions are individual – what works for one person does not necessarily work for another.

Financial Management

35 It is incumbent upon every family to plan for their financial future and save up money to cover future needs.

36 Every drop adds up, and every little bit of money saved or earned is significant.

37 No person is perfect and no budget is perfect. Financial failure is a learning experience, not a reason to give up or abandon a budget.

38 No financial plan can be executed to perfection. But that is not a reason not to plan.

39 Financial management has to be based on the current situation as well as data from the past and future projections. But it cannot be based on nostalgia for the past or wishful thinking about the future.

40 Husband and wife have to work as a team in managing their finances and should not conceal financial information from one another.

41 Writing down budgetary data contributes to budgetary control and discipline and is a powerful financial management tool.

Children & Money

42 Children and teenagers need to have the security of knowing that their parents will provide all of their needs.

43 Children's needs are subjective, and depend very much on their environment.

44 Children do not need to know the details of what is happening with their parents' finances. The only time children should be made aware of what is happening with their parents' finances is when there is a change in the family's lifestyle that will affect them directly.

45 Money is a potent, intoxicating, and dangerous substance whose use by young children needs to be supervised and controlled.

46 The less involved parents are in their married children's finances, the better it is for everyone.

47 Supporting adult children is noble, but better than any money parents can give their adult children is the gift of financial independence.

STUDENT RESOURCE 1

MESILA'S GUIDELINES FOR FINANCIAL STABILITY

EXERCISE

INSTRUCTIONS: EACH OF THE FOLLOWING 20 SCENARIOS REFLECTS AN ATTITUDE THAT MIGHT LEAD TO FINANCIAL INSTABILITY. FOR EACH SCENARIO, CHOOSE ONE OF MESILA'S GUIDELINES FOR FINANCIAL STABILITY THAT YOU WOULD SUGGEST TO THE PERSON IN THE SCENARIO. NEXT TO EACH SCENARIO, WRITE THE NUMBER OF THE RELEVANT GUIDELINE.

1 | Mendy needs to make some cuts to his budget. He considers cutting out the coffee that he buys each morning, but then he thinks to himself, *Why should I bother? What difference is $2 a day going to make?* ?

2 | Ephraim is worried that his friend Aaron is falling further and further into debt because of financial mismanagement, and he suggests that Aaron apply to Mesila for help. When Aaron balks at the suggestion, Ephraim goes ahead and applies on his behalf. *Once the process has begun, Aaron will cooperate*, he thinks to himself. ?

3 | Esther sees an advertisement that says: "Work from home, two hours a day, earn up to $10,000 a month. No training or experience necessary. Just call 999-5555." ?

4 | Mr. Rosen works very hard as an accountant, putting in late hours and sweating over his clients' tax returns. "I must be doing something wrong," he says. "It shouldn't be this hard to earn a living." ?

5 | Elimelech and Rochel are a young couple whose generous parents have given them a credit card to use for all of their expenses, with no limitations and no questions asked. ?

6 | Yaakov's brother Refoel is a big spender who has amassed a large debt on his credit card. Yaakov decides to pay off Refoel's debt in order to give him a fresh start.

7 | Rivky is a secretary who is earning a bit more than minimum wage. She has been at the same position for almost ten years, and is satisfied with her job and her pay.

8 | Chaim is worried that his wife Dina will be upset if he tells her the details of their financial situation. He decides not to discuss it with her at all.

9 | "I don't understand why I run out of money every month," Simcha tells his Mesila counselor. "I'm earning $4,000, and spending $3,000, so why should I be having problems?"

10 | The Rosenberg family decides that in order to balance their budget, they will get rid of their cars and their cell phones and will not buy any new clothing for at least two years.

11 | Yossi opens a new business, without preparing a business plan, hiring a business consultant, or performing any market research. When his friend comments that he is being irresponsible, Yossi replies, "I have *bitachon* that Hashem will take care of the business for me."

12 | Avraham and Baila are an affluent couple who give their children whatever they ask for. "We can afford it, *baruch Hashem*," they say.

13 | Zev has been unemployed for a long time, and his savings have run out. He borrows money from a *gemach* to cover his living expenses, not knowing how he is going to pay it back. "It's better than accepting *tzedakah*," he says.

14 | "Just because everyone else in your class has that type of knapsack does not mean that you need it," Mrs. Gold tells her daughter. "I grew up without it, and you'll manage just fine without it, too."

?

15 | Yitzchak and Esty decide that it's silly to build a budget plan, because they have no way of knowing what their financial situation will be in the future. "A person never knows what will happen tomorrow," they say. "How do we know how much we'll be earning or spending in six months from now?"

?

16 | Berel tells his neighbor Avigdor that he managed to build a budget plan that solved all of his financial problems. "Can I have a copy of your plan?" Avigdor asks. "I'll follow it exactly."

?

17 | Bracha's boss gives her an unexpected raise. "Now we'll be able to trade in the car for a newer model," she tells her husband happily. "And we'll finally be able to finish the month."

?

18 | Yerachmiel was a successful businessman whose store was severely affected by the economic crisis, but he feels uncomfortable asking experienced businesspeople for advice.

?

19 | Mrs. Ehrlich is a widow with several young children who subsists off community support. "I would love to manage without *tzedakah*," she says, "but I know that's impossible. What point is there in trying to minimize the amount of *tzedakah* I take?"

?

20 | Avrummy has nothing to do during bein hazmanim. "Why should anyone want to give me a job?" he laments. "I have no skills and never did well in school."

?

STUDENT RESOURCE 2

MASLOW'S HIERARCHY OF NEEDS

(MODIFIED)

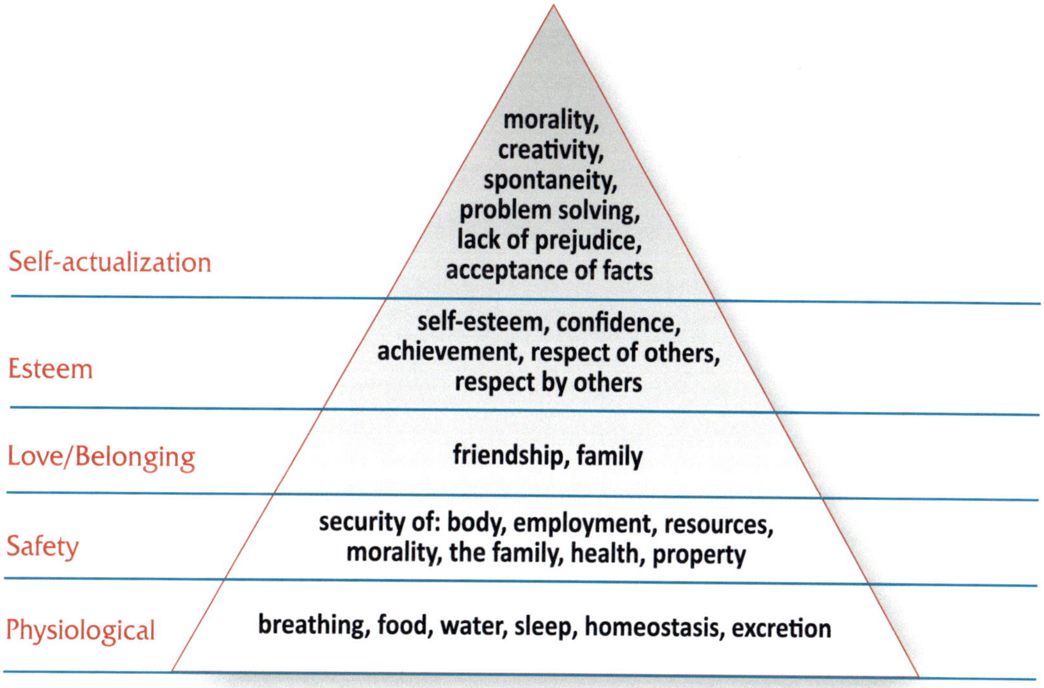

STUDENT RESOURCE 3

FIFTEEN HUNDRED DOLLAR EYE GLASSES:

A SHORTSIGHTED PROPOSITION?

Q: *I live in an affluent community, and although everyone has been affected to some extent by the economic downturn, I have not noticed any marked reduction in people's standard of living. The younger generation certainly does not seem to be feeling the pinch.*

Not long ago, my teenaged son asked me to buy him a pair of designer eyeglass frames priced at $1,500. When I told him that I thought $1,500 was outrageous for a pair of glasses, he told me that his friends are wearing glasses that are even more costly. I could not argue with that – his friends have expensive taste and their parents barely restrict their spending.

Although I am not as well-to-do as some of the parents of these boys, I can afford to buy my son the glasses he wants. Should I buy them for him?

A: In a recent column, we discussed why there is a need for Mesila nowadays, considering that our parents and grandparents managed very nicely without Mesila. We said that times have changed, and the realities of today are completely different from the realities people lived with even a generation ago.

Your question is a perfect example of why Mesila is needed today. Forty years ago, even twenty years ago, this question could not have existed. But today it is an important and relevant one.

Like any *chinuch* question, this one depends on many factors, not all of which are spelled out in your letter. One factor to consider: How many of your son's friends are wearing these designer glasses – 20%, 50%, or 90%? Another factor to consider: How is your overall relationship with your son? If you say "no" to him, will he be able to accept that without questioning your love and concern for him? And a third factor: Is your son going through a difficult time in his life?

If only a few of your son's friends are wearing these glasses, if your relationship with him is generally good, and if he is not experiencing any particular difficulty right now, then there are a number of reasons why spending $1,500 on glasses might not be wise.

With $1,500, you can buy glasses for an entire family, or feed a poor family for several weeks. To spend that kind of money on glasses will either cause the glasses to take on inflated significance, or it will reduce the value of $1,500 in your son's eyes. Neither of those options represents good *chinuch*.

We are not saying that people who have money should not spend it on themselves. Quite the contrary – if Hashem gave you money, you should appreciate and enjoy the gift He has given you. But even when spending money that you can afford to spend, you should not go overboard and lose all perspective of the value you are acquiring with your money. What value will you acquire by spending $1,500 on glasses that you would not acquire if you spent $50, $100, or $200? Will your son see any better, look any better, or be more comfortable in these glasses? We doubt it. Chances are, the only added value you would be getting is the designer label. If so, why would you pay $1,500 to provide free advertising for a company in Paris, Milan, or New York whose merchandise is grossly overpriced?

Then there is the question of sensitivity to the *tzibbur* – i.e., your son's peer group. There is already peer pressure among your son's friends to wear designer eyeglasses, as evidenced by your son's desire to buy them. If your son begins wearing these glasses, it will only reinforce the trend and intensify the peer pressure on those boys whose parents cannot afford to spend $1,500 on glasses. That may be insensitive, especially at a time when the entire world is experiencing an *eis tzarah*, a time of economic distress.

It is always prudent to avoid conspicuous consumption (see *Biur Halachah, Hilchos Yom Tov* 529:1), but during an *eis tzarah* there is even more reason to avoid it. Flaunting the fact that you are still able to spend money freely might make you vulnerable to *ayin hara* – and this is something that cannot be remedied by tying a red string to your son's glasses.

Beyond these considerations, buying your son $1,500 glasses sets a dangerous precedent by introducing him to a level of spending that may be unsustainable. While he might be happy with the glasses now, he may be very *un*happy in the future if he has to go back to the kind of glasses worn by the proletariat. And once he sees that it is acceptable to spend $1,500 on glasses, he will likely want to spend similar amounts of money on other items that he wants.

In the not-too-distant future, your son will be married, *b'ezras Hashem*, and who knows if he and his wife will be able to keep up the level of spending you have conditioned him to? For that matter, who knows if *you* will be able to maintain this level of spending? We are not wishing hardship on anyone, but if there is one lesson to learn from the current economic crisis it is that no one's financial future is certain. Spending so much money on glasses is therefore shortsighted (pardon the pun), and might ultimately be a major disservice to your son.

Even if you were a billionaire and you could be reasonably certain that your son would always be able to afford $1,500 glasses, it would still be in your son's best interests to experience the disappointment of not getting things he wants. The Steipler Gaon said that the reason that so many people today are unhappy and depressed is because they never lacked anything when they were growing up, so they never developed coping skills to deal with disappointment. They therefore fall apart when they are confronted with life's inevitable disappointments.

Life's disappointments can be much worse than not getting $1,500 glasses, and these disappointments often happen in areas of life where money is useless. You would not want your son to fall apart if he is not accepted to the yeshiva of his choice or if he is turned down during the shidduchim process, and the best way to prepare him for these possible disappointments is in the training ground of eyeglasses and other minor letdowns.

The higher people's expectations are, the more likely they are to be disappointed when those expectations are not met. There is a danger, therefore, in indulging wants, whether our children's or our own. Each time we say "yes" to a child's want, we reinforce it and turn it into more of a need. Conversely, each time we deny our children something they want, we teach them to want less.

But this is true only of wants, not of needs. Needs, if unmet, only become more intense and lead to feelings of deprivation. To illustrate: if a person is hungry and does not yield to the urge to eat, he will only become hungrier, because he has a real need for food. But if a person wants chocolate and does not give in to the urge, eventually his desire for chocolate will abate and it will become easier for him to resist the temptation.

Because needs tend to intensify with time and wants tend to abate, a good way to determine whether a child's request represents a need or a want is to see what happens when you say no: is the child able to forget about the item after a few days, or does he continue asking for it incessantly?

If your son *needs* the glasses – and it is possible that he does – then you should consider getting them for him, because otherwise, he will feel deprived and his craving for the glasses will intensify. But if he only *wants* the glasses, then his initial disappointment at not getting them will fade quickly, and he will be a stronger, happier person for the experience. Stronger, because he has learned how to handle disappointment, and happier, because his expectations have been lowered and it is therefore easier for him to be content.

It is normal for children – and adults – to want things, especially things that their friends have. Before dismissing your son's request as outrageous or frivolous, it is important to understand *why* he wants the glasses and empathize with his desire. Once you understand why he wants them, you can look together for alternative ways to satisfy the hunger underlying his desire. That hunger may be for attention, for social acceptance, or for a boost to his self-image. If you sincerely try to understand your son's desire for designer glasses, you may be pleasantly surprised to realize that "yes" and "no" are not your only two options. Between $1,500 glasses and nothing, there is plenty of middle ground, plenty of room for flexibility. Another idea would be for him to shop around and try to find similar eyewear at a more reasonable price. There are many other ways to make both him and you happy – the key is to put yourself into a mindset of consideration, rather than opposition, and chances are that he will follow suit.

If you are in such a mindset, then even if you decide not to buy him the glasses, you will be able to cushion the "no" with understanding, compassion and love so that he can accept it without anger or resentment.

In summary, we recommend that you carefully consider the pros and cons of buying your son the glasses, evaluate whether his request represents a need or a want, identify the hunger underlying the request, and look for a way to satisfy that hunger without compromising your values or your relationship.

After you consider the general guidelines we have offered, we suggest that you consult with a *chinuch* expert in order to receive specific guidance for your situation.

STUDENT RESOURCE 4

THIS IS YOUR BRAIN ON EASY CREDIT

How did Americans rack up $11.83 trillion in debt? Short term rewards light up the brain's emotional system.

The reward circuitry of the human brain is vital to our survival, but it wasn't built to grapple with seductive credit card offers and no-money-down mortgages. Easy credit feeds our love of immediate gratification, distorts self-regulation and diminishes prudent market behavior, creating a destabilizing positive-feedback loop. Analysts trying to understand the explosion of consumer debt should look no further than neuroscience.

The total indebtedness of U.S. households at the end of last year stood at $11.83 trillion, the Federal Reserve Bank of New York has estimated. That's up by $117 billion from the previous quarter. Credit card balances rose by $20 billion, auto loans by $21 billion, and student loans by a startling $31 billion. Falling indebtedness after the financial meltdown of 2008 was due largely to default rather than repayment. Now as restrictions on credit are easing, debt levels have begun to climb again

Easy credit as an economic driver has become a Faustian bargain. A market ethos that feeds on short-term desire, low interest rates and tax systems that encourage borrowing has distorted consumer choice. But more than that, it has upended the ancient survival game our brains use to weigh risk and reward.

At the core, we are instinctively selfish creatures, focused on the short term and driven by habit. The twin frontal lobes of the brain, which sit above the eye sockets, are the brain's "executive" cortex, overseeing risk assessment. Kaleidoscopic streams of incoming information are integrated there with past knowledge and instinctual drive.

A conscious, deliberative "thinking" cycle, drawing heavily on memory, runs through the outer cortex, the region predominantly concerned with punishment and control. An "emotional" circuit, focused on reward and pleasure, operates in the same region, but internally.

In their crosstalk, these parallel cycles of perception and action create a balance between the fear of pain or loss and the expectation of pleasure or profit.

The illusion of continuous economic growth and the explosion of credit have thrown that balance out of whack. Thanks to the seductive appeal of today's consumer economy, perhaps for the first time in human history it is the affirmation of reward rather than the fear of punishment or failure that dominates the calculus of risk. We have become addicted to the quick fix, be that tasty junk food, the electronic cocaine of the Internet, or the painless ease of a credit card purchase.

Research demonstrates that when presented with a choice between a reward now and a greater one after a delay—for instance, $80 today or $100 in two weeks—many of us will opt for the cash in hand, despite its lesser value. Scientists call this temporal discounting. Imaging studies using MRIs show that thinking about an immediate reward lights up the brain's limbic system, which regulates emotion. Thus passion prevails over reason. That area of the brain is quieter when we're considering a reward in the distant future, and thus logic wins out. Would you rather have $80 in one year, or $100 in a year plus two weeks? The question answers itself.

Though Wall Street and international financiers have been cast as the villains of the 2008 madness, they are minor actors in the larger narrative of spendthrift habit in which we each played our part.

In the past three decades, aided and abetted by the enticements of consumerism, we Americans have been busily retuning our neural architecture.

During the last 25 years of the 20th century, the U.S. economy was in recession only 5% of the time, compared with 22% of the previous quarter-century. Such long periods of uninterrupted growth reflexively foster a mood of complacency: Secure in our habits we have learned to be thoughtless. We have disrupted the autopilots of the brain's internal market, resetting the balance between hedonism and prudent self-constraint. Passion has prevailed over reason.

If we are to reset ourselves, the building of character will be key. As Adam Smith recognized, character is not born but crafted through thoughtful self-command. Ideally, over time a man becomes his own best critic, creating in the mind an intuitive capacity to monitor personal thoughts and actions. This facility Smith personified as the Impartial Spectator, moderating the perennial struggle between passion and reason.

Yet the habits of prudent concern and

self-command develop, just as do profligate habits, through social exchange. Ask who is responsible for the development of character and there is no single answer, because it is a collective responsibility. It is regrettable that discussion of how good character is built has become an unfashionable subject, largely ignored in today's public debate. In such company, addicted to the short-term and too shy to consider the virtues that underpin civil society, easy credit finds its rightful place. Neuroscience suggests it's time to put impulse aside and to consider the longer view. To think for a few days before making that big purchase may offer a running start.

Questions:

1. What is the *"ancient survival game"* the article refers to?
2. In your own words what has *"upended the ancient survival game"* and how has it done so?
3. What is *"temporal discounting"*?
4. Explain: *"Americans have been busily retuning our neural architecture…"* How have our brains been rewired in recent history causing a lowering of human behavior?
5. What is *"thoughtful self command"*?
6. What is this author's suggestion to stop impulsive spending? Explain.

Dr. Whybrow is director of the Semel Institute for Neuroscience and Human Behavior at UCLA and the author of "The Well-Tuned Brain: Neuroscience and the Life Well Lived" (out May 18 from W.W. Norton), from which this op-ed is adapted.

STUDENT RESOURCE 5

FINANCIAL INSTABILITY: **NO ONE IS IMMUNE**

Let's look at a crisis that hit one of the wealthiest Jewish communities in the world

Following is a speech given by Ike Sutton, president of an organization called the Sephardic Angel Fund, whose goal is to teach responsible budgeting habits to the Brooklyn Syrian Jewish community.
These are excerpts from a speech he gave at a fundraising event some years back:

Good Morning:

Thank you for permitting me to speak to you today. In the few short years that the Sephardic Angel Fund has been helping people in our community, we have learned quite a bit about the demographics and dynamics of our community.

I would like to share four main facts with you this morning about what we have learned and how this knowledge has strengthened our resolve to further our efforts. I believe that if you are informed, you too will want to be part of this opportunity to help our fellow Jews.

Fact 1:

Imagine, if you will, that there is a chart behind me. At one end of the chart, we see 10% of our community. They are the wealthiest members of our kehillah. They spend as they like and have plenty saved. May G-d continue to bless them with the prosperity they enjoy.

At the opposite end of the chart is another 10%. They are the budget-minded members of our community. They spend what they earn, whether it is $30,000 or $300,000, and live within their means. They have no debt and do not overspend in the least.

The middle of the chart represents the remaining 80% of our community. They live way beyond their means, spending much more than they make. They are juggling 6-8 credit cards and making only minimum payments on them; they have a second and a third mortgage on their homes; and they have borrowed money from at least a dozen friends and family members.

Fact 2:

This 80% group falls into two categories:

1. those who spend to keep up with the Joneses

and

2. those who are burdened by 3 major components of their personal budgets. They are:

> *a. The average cost of a mortgage today is between $4,000 and $5,000 a month. Over a year's time, that amounts to $60,000 for housing alone.*
>
> *b. The average annual costs for tuition and camp for a family with four children is another $60,000, maybe even more.*
>
> *c. When you include an estimated cost of $20,000 per year for utilities and insurance, you are already up to $140,000—and that's after tax dollars.*

That means you would have to earn at least $200,000 before taxes—and you didn't even begin to include expenses for food, clothing, medical bills, or a car. To cover those costs, you would have to earn well over $300,000 at a minimum.

At our Career Services Division, we are placing hundreds of people each year in positions with salaries ranging from $30,000 to $150,000. When is the last time you knew of someone getting a job for $300,000? Most of the people in this 80% demographic aren't qualified to land a job at even $100,000.

Fact 3: Our Youth

We took a look at a typical 18-year-old boy in our community. He has graduated from high school and figures that he can go to work and get a job for maybe $500 or $600 a week. That sounds like a lot of money to him.

He doesn't have the slightest idea about taxes. He hasn't figured out how credit cards really work. He has no experience with making or sticking to a budget.

In addition, he's not sure that he really wants to go to college because going to school for another four years means he won't be able to go to work and earn any money. And of course he needs money…

On top of all that, his parents absolutely are not cool. He can't talk to them at all about anything. They're old-fashioned, behind the times, and simply do not understand him—and they never will.

Fact 4: Newly Married Couples

Our analysis of this demographic also indicates that in four years' time these kids will be getting married, and they won't be any smarter about taxes or credit or any other issues because nobody is preparing them to be the husbands and wives, the mothers and fathers, the business leaders of tomorrow.

They have no idea about what it means to be married. They have no understanding of the financial obligations of a married couple because they had no understanding of finances to begin with…

They lack the most fundamental information about money and marriage and being a part of a community. And of course, they haven't the slightest inkling about what it means to…raise a child together, to educate and provide everything for that child for years to come. Why? Because no one has taught them about those things either.

And that's the real tragedy. They won't be any more prepared to teach their children than their parents were. And the cycle will repeat itself over and over again.

Sounds bleak, doesn't it? It is, and it will only get worse as the community expands. Estimates are that in 25 years, our community will double its numbers. In other words, even more families will be struggling to cope, to make ends meet, to get from one month to the next, from one paycheck to the next.

At the Angel Fund, we feel we have a solution to this problem, a cure-all for this "illness," in which 80% of our community is living beyond their means.

It is not our job to tell anyone how much they should spend for their homes, their cars, their weddings, and bar mitzvahs. It is not our place to tell people how to live. If they can afford it, they are entitled to enjoy it.

In the old days, people used to walk around with coins in their pocket, and that's how they paid for whatever they wanted. If something they wanted cost 40 coins, and if they had only 20 coins, they would save until they had the coins they needed.

Today people don't have the foggiest idea about how much money they have. Their paychecks are automatically deposited. They use plastic credit cards to buy what they want without even knowing their credit limits. They can easily borrow money from the bank by putting their homes up as collateral. And it's all done electronically. They never see their money, they never feel their money, and they can never really get a handle on what they have.

Our solution is to institute a modern-day coin system, and that is called budgeting with a pencil and paper. Our first step is to make a family unit aware of what moneys are coming in and what moneys are going out. Once our family unit is aware and can actually see how their money is being spent, they can collectively address their financial problems and seek solutions.

This speech could have been given to **any Jewish community in the world** – perhaps with different numbers, but the principles are equally relevant.

The lifestyles described may be wealthy by objective standards – but do they *feel* wealthy? Aren't they struggling to pay their $5,000 mortgages the same way some poor Israeli families are struggling to pay their $500 mortgages? Mesila's tools enable people to avoid this kind of financial stress – whether they're Syrian, chassidish, yeshivish, modern, or anything else.

STUDENT RESOURCE 6

WALLPAPERING YOUR HOUSE WITH SHAS

The Chofetz Chaim's Advice for Maximizing the Use of Your Assets

Source #1: *Sefer Shem Olam (by the Chofetz Chaim) 1:13*

והנה כאשר נתבונן היטב במעשינו, נמצא שבעוה"ר דפי הש"ס פרושים אצלנו על כתלי הבית, וכן דפי המשניות על הכסאות היפים והשולחנות הנאים, וכן ההלכות שבתורה פרושים על בגדינו היפים והבגדים היפים של כל אנשי ביתנו. ולא תאמר כי ממשיל משלים אנוכי, אראה לעיני הקורא את בירור דברי.

דהנה במדרש משלי פרק עשירי איתא, ששואלין לו לאדם בעת הדין על הכל, דהיינו על מקרא ועל משנה ועל הלכות ועוד כמה עניינים עי"ש. והנה כיון ששואלין לו לאדם על הכל, מסתמא ניתן לו לאדם דעת מתחילה שיוכל להשיג הכל, וכאשר יתבונן האדם בעצמו בימי חייו יראה בעצמו שכמעט הוא חסר מכל זה, ואף אם הוא יודע במקצת, ידיעתו מועטה מאד בש"ס וכן במשניות ומדרש וכדומה. וכאשר ירצה בעצמו להבין סיבת הדבר אנה הלכו כוחותיו וזמן ימי חייו, ימצא שהחליף את הש"ס שלו [דהיינו הכוחות והדעת שניתן לו על זה] בדירה נאה של כמה חדרים, וכן המשניות וההלכות על בגדים יפים לו ולכל אנשי ביתו בכל ימי חייו, הרי לך בירור דברינו שכוחותינו שניתנו לנו להשיג תורתנו הקדושה שבכתב ושבעל פה הם כעת פרושים על הכתלים והכסאות וכדומה, שהחלפנו בסכלותנו עולם עומד בעולם עובר, ונתקיים בנו מה שאמר הכתוב אכלו זרים כחו והוא לא ידע, דהיינו כח החמדה והתאוה והכעס כילו כל כוחותיו על דבר של הבל והוא לא התבונן על האונאה הגדולה שיש בהמסחר הזה, והרי אנו דומים במעשינו בעוונותינו הרבים לפראים שבאפריקא שמחליפים כסף וזהב באיזה פרחים של מיני צעצועים:

[ספר שם עולם (להחפץ חיים) - חלק א' פרק י"ג]

Source #2:
Sefer Sfas Tamim
(by the Chofetz Chaim) ch. 5

בענין זה, שבתחלה כשהקב"ה מזמין לאדם מעות בחסדו, כדי שיוכל להחיות את נפשו בזה, וגם לפרוע מזה חובות הבורא כצדקה וגמ"ח והחזקת התורה, וכדומה לזה. היצה"ר מסיתו, שעתה נאות לו להתנהג בענייני הוצאות הבית והמלבושים במעלה הגבוה מערכו והפחות כהמכובד, והמכובד כאחד מעשירי העם...

[ספר שפת תמים (להחפץ חיים) - פרק ה']

Source #3: *Sefer Chofetz Chaim*

כָּל מַה שֶּׁהַקָּדוֹשׁ בָּרוּךְ הוּא יוֹסִיף לוֹ בְּטוֹבָה וְיַרְוִיחַ לוֹ בַּעֲסָקָיו יוֹתֵר, יְסִיתֶנּוּ הַיֵּצֶר לֵאמֹר, כִּי עַתָּה לְפִי עָשְׁרְךָ שֶׁנָּתַן לְךָ הַקָּדוֹשׁ בָּרוּךְ הוּא, אַתָּה מֻכְרָח לָדוּר בְּדִירָה נָאָה יוֹתֵר וְלֵילֵךְ בְּמַלְבּוּשֵׁי רִקְמָה וּלְהִתְנַהֵג כְּדֶרֶךְ בַּעֲלֵי הַבָּתִּים הַגְּבוֹהִים, שֶׁאִם לֹא כֵן תִּתְבַּזֶּה לְעֵינֵי חֲבֵרֶיךָ, וְלָכֵן אַתָּה מֻכְרָח עַתָּה לְבַטֵּל בַּפַּעַם הַזֹּאת אֶת הַקְּבִיעוּת עִתִּים לַתּוֹרָה שֶׁלְּךָ וְלִסַּע לְמָקוֹם פְּלוֹנִי וּפְלוֹנִי לְהַרְוִיחַ.

[ספר חפץ חיים - פתיחה, עשין]

STUDENT RESOURCE 7

LIFE INSURANCE: TO BUY OR NOT TO BUY?

By Rabbi Yirmiyohu Kaganoff

In Parshas Vayishlach, Yaakov needed to make very important and practical life decisions with major long-term ramifications, when he heard that Esav was approaching with his army of 400 men; these decisions were made based on his halachic and hashkafic background. We also have similar decisions to make. With this introduction, I bring you:

Question 1

Chaim knows that, as the head of the family, he has the responsibility to care for his wife, Fruma, and their children. He feels that this responsibility obligates him to acquire an adequate amount of life insurance should something *chas veshalom* happen to him. Fruma's upbringing was that even discussing this matter can cause bad things to happen. Who is right – Chaim or Fruma?

Question 2

Miriam calls her *rav* with a *shaylah*. "My husband and I would like to buy life insurance, but we're concerned that it might show a lack of bitachon that Hashem always does what is best for us. Is that correct?"

* Reprinted with permission from the author.

Question 3

Tzadok is one of the city's biggest *tzaddikim*. He teaches, voluntarily oversees some local *tzedakah* projects, not to mention his incredibly solid *kevi'us itim*. He is a *talmid chacham* and is raising his own large family. One of the *ba'alei batim* has offered to purchase a life insurance policy on his behalf, but Tzadok questions whether doing so might jeopardize him, since his family would no longer be dependent on his support. Is his fear founded?

Answer:

At times we have heard someone opposing life insurance, claiming that it reflects a lack of *bitachon*, or that its acquisition could actually be to one's detriment. Let us understand what the halachic authorities say about this subject. Indeed, are there halachic or hashkafic concerns about purchasing life insurance? From a Torah perspective, should this practice be encouraged or discouraged?

The three situations I presented above demonstrate three different issues that *poskim* discuss when analyzing whether there is a halachic problem in purchasing life insurance. They are:

I. Creating a Devil's Advocate

The *Gemara* states that one should not say something that might cause evil to occur. *Al yiftach adam piv l'satan* – Do not create an opportunity for Satan to mix in! Is purchasing life insurance not considered encouraging the evil Satan to do something nefarious?

II. In G-d We Trust

If we really believe that Hashem provides for all of our needs, doesn't purchasing life insurance demonstrate that we are worried about the future and lack trust in Hashem?

III. Succeeding in Divine Judgment

As opposed to a human court, Hashem's judgment and decisions are perfect, and take all ramifications into consideration. The Heavenly Tribunal will not recall someone unless all the consequences of his disappearance are calculated. Based on this, perhaps purchasing life insurance jeopardizes the insured, since his family is no longer as dependent on his support, thus minimizing the merits he has when judged by the Heavenly Tribunal?

Let's analyze each one of these issues individually, in order to determine whether or not purchasing life insurance should be allowed or even encouraged.

Issue #1: Creating a Devil's Advocate

Al yiftach adam piv l'satan literally translates as, "A person should not open his mouth for Satan." One should be careful not to say something that might provide Satan with ammunition. The *Gemara* applies this rule to forbid a person from saying, "I sinned a lot, but *Hashem* has not punished me." The admission that one is guilty and deserves punishment gives Satan a chance to prosecute one in the Heavenly Tribunal. According to the *Magen Avraham*, the main concern here is that the words "*Hashem* has not punished me" imply that one anticipates the punishment, although this is clearly not what the speaker intends. However, when Satan prosecutes, he might take the speaker's words out of context.

The question is whether purchasing life insurance provides Satan with such an opportunity to prosecute.

A different Talmudic discussion implies that it is absolutely permissible to make arrangements for oneself in the event of one's demise, and that doing so is not considered opening one's mouth to Satan. The *Gemara* discusses whether someone who prepares for himself shrouds (*tachrichim*) that are four-cornered is required to attach *tzitzis* to their corners, implying that it is, indeed, permitted to prepare shrouds for oneself. In other words, planning for one's death does not constitute violating the warning *al yiftach adam piv l'satan* and does not provide the Satan with any ammunition.

Indeed, this *Gemara's* discussion is rallied as a source in the following situation. Maury Bond is lying on his deathbed on a hot Friday afternoon. There is concern that if he dies before Shabbos, his corpse will begin to decompose and smell unpleasant before it can be buried after Shabbos, which would not be a *kavod* for the departed. (Remember that earlier generations did not have ready access to refrigeration.) The authorities debate whether it is permitted to dig Maury's grave while he is still breathing, so that, should he die on Friday, he could be buried quickly before Shabbos. Most authorities permit digging the grave while Maury is still living; the dissenting opinion prohibits this out of concern that Maury might find out that his grave is already dug, which will distress him, and this itself could lead to his premature demise. However, none of the authorities debating this case is concerned that the efficacy of digging Maury's grave while he is still alive violates *al yiftach adam piv l'satan* and provides Satan with the opportunity to clamor for Maury's swift departure. Some of the authorities who discuss this question explicitly state that it is perfectly acceptable for a healthy person to arrange the digging of his own grave and to prepare his own shrouds, as we see from the above-quoted passage in the *Gemara*. One highly respected authority expressly approves the practice of purchasing adjacent burial plots for a couple, the fact that at least one member is still alive notwithstanding.

Thus, we see that it is not considered *al yiftach adam piv l'satan* when a healthy person makes funeral arrangements for himself, since he is not mentioning his sins and giving Satan any reason to prosecute him. Based on this, several authorities rule that purchasing life insurance is also not a violation of *al yiftach adam piv l'satan*.

However, I would like to note that there are two sources from which it seems that *al yiftach adam piv l'satan* applies in some other cases. In *Kesubos* 8b, the *Gemara* states that a person should not make the following declaration, "Many will drink the cup of mourning" because of the concern of *al yiftach adam piv l'satan*. This source implies that there is concern of *al yiftach adam piv l'satan* even when one's statement does not imply that one has sinned and deserves punishment. Similarly, a different *Gemara* passage states that upon entering the bathhouse (which in those days involved a moderate degree of danger), one should not say, "if something goes wrong, my death should atone for my sins", because of *al yiftach adam piv l'satan*.

Thus, we need to resolve why the halachic authorities who discuss making shrouds, digging a grave, or purchasing a burial plot for a living person do not prohibit these actions because of the principle of *al yiftach adam piv l'satan*, even though the statements, "many will drink the cup of mourning" and "if something goes wrong, my death should atone for my sins", are prohibited for this reason.

The answer appears to be that these last two cases are a concern only because one is ***expressing*** the possibility of one's passing, which fits the words of *Chazal*: a person should not *say*, "I sinned a lot, but *Hashem* has not punished me."

Assuming our solution is correct, arranging plans for one's demise, including writing one's will and purchasing life insurance would not violate *al yiftach adam piv l'satan*, provided that one does not express verbally the possibility of one's death.

Issue #2:

In G-d We Trust – Exclusively

A Jew is obligated to believe that although he makes an effort to earn his livelihood (parnassah), it is ultimately Hashem alone Who provides it. The question is whether there is a difference between working for one's daily needs and working to save money for future expenses. Is it a shortcoming in *bitachon* to save for the future? Does purchasing life insurance imply lack of confidence that Hashem will provide for his family?

To answer these questions, we must first examine the halachic relationship between *parnassah* and *bitachon*.

Is there a Dispute in the Mishnah?

The Mishnah quotes two ostensibly dissenting opinions. Rabbi Meir is quoted first as saying: "A person should teach his son a livelihood that is easy (to learn) and free of potential sin. (At the same time, he should) pray to Him Who is the source of all wealth and property. (Always realize that) there is no profession that does not have its vicissitudes. Poverty and wealth are dependent on his merit." We see that Rabbi Meir advocates teaching one's child a livelihood, while simultaneously acknowledging that livelihood comes from Hashem and not from our efforts.

On the other hand, the very same mishnah quotes Rabbi Nehorai as saying, "I abandon all means of livelihood and teach my son only Torah."

Thus, we appear to have a dispute between two *tanna'im* as to whether one should take time from teaching one's son Torah in order to provide him with vocational training. However, this analysis cannot be accurate for the following reason:

The *Gemara* teaches that Rabbi Meir was an alternate name for Rabbi Nehorai, because his teaching of Torah produced so much light. (Meir means "He who gives light," and the word Nehorai also means "light".) How could Rabbi Nehorai disagree with himself?

Resolving the Dispute

One answer to this problem is that Rabbi Nehorai's statement that he would teach his son nothing but Torah was personal – Rabbi Nehorai himself had no worldly concerns, because he placed complete trust in Hashem. Someone at this level should indeed not teach his son any worldly occupation. However, most people do not reach this level of trust and must provide their son with a livelihood, while emphasizing that *parnassah* is from Hashem.

Rav Moshe Feinstein presents an alternative answer to the contradictory statements of Rabbi Meir. The two statements are discussing different stages of life, one before the son must begin supporting his family, and the other when he has to support his family. Rabbi Nehorai's statement that "I teach my son only Torah" applies before the son needs *parnassah*. Until then, he should learn only Torah. The other statement refers to a son who has to earn a living. At that point, his father should teach him a livelihood that involves few halachic challenges and is easy to learn, while at the same time teaching him that his vocation is only *hishtadlus*, one's feeble apparent attempt, and that *parnassah* comes only from Hashem.

There is a halachic difference between the two approaches. According to the first approach, someone with total trust that Hashem will provide for him, even if he makes no *hishtadlus*, should not make any effort toward *parnassah*. According to Rav Moshe's approach, even a person with total trust in Hashem is required to have a livelihood. Rav Moshe brings evidence from several sources that it is inappropriate to rely on miracles for one's *parnassah*. Furthermore, he considers having no livelihood as equivalent to relying on miracles.

On the other hand, Rav Vozner rules, similarly to the first approach, that a pure *baalbitachon* is permitted to rely totally on Hashem for *parnassah*; however, he agrees that this applies only to rare individuals. There are stories about *Gedolim*, such as Rav Yosef Chayim Sonnenfeld, who made no conventional *hishtadlus* to attain *parnassah*. These *Gedolim*, too, must have had the same opinion as Rav Vozner. According to Rav Moshe's approach, one may not deliberately adopt such a lifestyle.

Both Rav Moshe and Rav Vozner rule that, generally speaking, people are required to have some type of *parnassah*, and that it is not a lack of *bitachon* to do so. Unless he is a great *tzaddik*, no one should assume that he has sufficient *zechuyos* (merits) to expect Hashem to provide his *parnassah* with no *hishtadlus* whatsoever on his part.

The *poskim* bring evidence from *Tosafos* that it is not a shortcoming to make arrangements to take care of one's financial future. The *Gemara* rules that although a father has the halachic ability to marry off his daughter while she is a minor, he is prohibited to do so out of concern that when she grows up, she may not like her husband. In the time of the *Tosafos*, however, underage daughters were married off, which appeared to be a violation of this halachah. Upon what basis was there a practice contrary to the *Gemara's* ruling?

Tosafos explains that in his turbulent times (the *Baalei Tosafos* lived during the period of the Crusades), a man who had sufficient means to provide his daughter with a dowry, should arrange her marriage to someone appropriate. If the father delayed, he risked losing his money, which could have been tantamount to his becoming unable to marry off his daughter. *Tosafos* does not contend that a person should have *bitachon* that he will have the means to be able to marry her off later.

Similarly, someone who can purchase life insurance, an annuity, or other means for making his life or the lives of his dependents more secure, may do so. *Bitachon* does not require someone to ignore future needs. *Bitachon* does require that a person realize that everything that happens is under Hashem's supervision and control.

What Will I Eat Tomorrow?

But doesn't this approach violate the statement that "Someone who has (today's) bread in his basket, and asks, 'What will I eat tomorrow?' lacks faith"? Aren't *Chazal* teaching us that someone who plans for tomorrow's livelihood lacks proper trust in Hashem?

The answer is no. This last passage is discussing people's beliefs. Everyone must believe that Hashem provides for him and that whatever happens is under His control. One may not say, "What will I eat tomorrow?" thereby ignoring Hashem's supervision. However, this does not mean that making practical plans for the future is a violation of *bitachon*, provided one fully realizes that everything comes from Hashem and is dependent on Him.

The Manna

However, there is another passage of *Gemara* that may indicate otherwise:

"Rabbi Shimon ben Yochai's disciples asked him, 'Why did the manna not fall for the *B'nei Yisrael* once a year (for the entire year)?' He answered them, 'I will give you a parable. A human king once provided his son with support on an annual basis. The son visited his father once a year to receive his allowance. Wanting to see his son more often, the father altered the system and began providing his son with support on a daily basis. Thereafter, his son visited his father every day. Similarly, the head of a large household worried that no manna would fall on the morrow; thus he would pray daily for sustenance." Doesn't this *Gemara* imply that it is better for one's *parnassah* to arrive one day at a time than to plan for the future?

The halachic authorities provide two answers to this question that are dependent on the dispute between Rav Vozner and Rav Moshe mentioned earlier. According to Rav Vozner, this *Gemara* reflects the ideal: a great *tzaddik* should indeed receive his *parnassah* one day at a time. However, most people are not at this level of faith and may plan for the future. According to Rav Moshe's approach, the *Gemara* means that a person should mentally acknowledge every day that Hashem provides for all his needs; however, he is permitted and required to make *hishtadlus*, which includes planning for future needs. It should be noted that all the *poskim* that I have seen discussing this issue rule that purchasing life insurance qualifies as normal *hishtadlus*.

In this context, it is worthwhile to quote a *Midrash* that demonstrates the obligation to make *hishtadlus*. Quoting the *pasuk*, "*L'ma'an yevorechecha Hashem Elokecha b'chol ma'asecha asher ta'aseh*," "So that Hashem Your G-d will bless you in all your deeds that you will perform," the *Midrash* points out that the last two words of the *posuk*, "*asher taaseh*," "that you will perform" are seemingly superfluous, because the Torah already stated, "*b'chol ma'asecha*," "in all your deeds." What is added with the words, "that you will perform?"

The *Midrash* explains, "The Torah states, 'Keep the mitzvos.' I might think that he should do nothing and expect his *parnassah* to come automatically?

Therefore, the Torah repeats, 'that you will perform.' If you work, you will receive blessing, and if you do not work, you will not receive blessing." This *Midrash* proves that one has a responsibility to earn *parnassah*.

Issue #3:
Succeeding in Divine Judgment

I have heard people give yet another reason why someone should not purchase life insurance. What happens if a husband does not have the personal merit to guarantee longevity, while his wife and children do have the merit or the *mazel* (fortune) to live financially secure lives? In a case like this, the husband would live a long productive life as their provider. By purchasing life insurance, which guarantees their sustenance even without his presence, he jeopardizes his life, since his dependents are now provided for should something bad happen to him.

In the one halachic source that I saw mention this concern, the author, Rav Yitzchok Sternhell *zt"l*, quoted the exact opposite approach in the name of the Shinaver Rav (Rav Yechezkel Shraga Halberstam *zt"l*, author of *Divrei Yechezkel*), who was one of the greatest halachic authorities of his day in Galicia. The Shinaver contended that buying life insurance should provide longevity. He argues that since the *mazel* of the people who own insurance companies is to become wealthy, their *mazel* will prevail and prevent them from losing money by having to pay out life insurance policies. Thus, purchasing a policy actually rallies *mazel* to one's side and does not jeopardize one's life.

Another counter-argument runs as follows: If loss of merit is a concern, then there is valid reason to refrain from accumulating any wealth. The family members of a man who ekes out a daily existence are far more dependent on their breadwinner than are the wife and children of a wealthy man, since he will leave them with an appreciable inheritance should something happen to him. Thus, one could argue that accumulating wealth is not in one's best interest, an approach that does not have too many advocates. I have never seen anyone refrain from accumulating wealth because of this concern, and neither have I seen any halachic authority suggest this as a reason to avoid affluence. Therefore, I conclude that this is not a factor in the question of purchasing life insurance.

In conclusion, I am aware of thirteen written *teshuvos* (responsa) on the purchase of life insurance or annuities, written by authorities representing *Litvishe, Chassidishe* and Sefardic approaches. All thirteen *teshuvos* permit purchasing life insurance, and some encourage the practice strongly.

Rav Meir Shapiro, the rosh yeshiva of Yeshivas Chachmei Lublin, had a very large life insurance policy, even though he unfortunately had no children. His reason was that since fundraising for the yeshiva was completely on his shoulders, he was concerned that in the event of his premature death, the yeshiva would be forced to close. We see that he was not concerned with any of the above issues and felt that purchasing insurance was an appropriate course of action. ***May we all be blessed with long years and good health.***

STUDENT RESOURCE 8

MAKING MILLIONS ON DINARS

Q: *A yungerman in the kollel where I learn recently showed me an article describing the exciting new possibility of investing in Iraqi dinars. The article said that until 1982, the Iraqi dinar was worth about $3, and today, one million Iraqi dinars can be bought for only $700. The value of the dinar is sure to rise when the conflict in Iraq is resolved, and my friends tell me that I can invest a few thousand dollars in Iraqi dinars and come out with millions of dollars when the dinar goes up. I have some money put aside that I was looking to invest. I know many yungeleit who have invested in these dinars, and I am wondering if I should do the same. Do you think this is a worthwhile investment?*

A: We at Mesila are not licensed investment advisors, and we are therefore not qualified to guide you with regard to the specifics of investments. For investment advice, we suggest that you contact a licensed financial professional such as Hamodia investment columnist Aaron Katsman, who happens to be an active Mesila volunteer counselor.

We also do not wish to discuss the issue of whether it is appropriate for a *ben Torah* to busy himself with investment opportunities, although we would certainly hope that your *kollel* studies focus on disputes between Abaye and Rava, not on the finer points of the conflict between the Shiites and the Sunnis.

Mesila's mission, and the objective of this column, is to convey responsible, Torah-based attitudes towards finances. We will therefore attempt to expose the fallacies inherent in get-rich-quick schemes, the Iraqi dinar craze in particular.

From the time Adam Harishon was cursed, "By the sweat of your brow shall you eat bread," earning a livelihood has been a struggle for mankind. There are no exemptions from this curse, and promises of easy money are always – *always* – misleading.

For someone learning in *kollel*, investing might seem like the ideal way to earn *parnassah* effortlessly, without ever having to leave the *beis medrash*. All you have to do is put your money into a surefire investment, and you are set. Well, it does not quite work that way.

Investing, by definition, means risking capital for the sake of an anticipated future gain, or return. As a rule, return is directly proportional to risk – the greater the risk, the higher the potential return. The converse is true as well: the higher the potential return, the greater the risk. If someone promises you returns of millions of dollars on an investment of thousands, you can be sure of two things: (1) the risk is far too high to justify the investment, and (2) the person is either very naïve or a con artist.

Get-rich-quick schemes lure people with the promise of high returns and no risk. But wise investors know that any investment that cannot go down, cannot go up either. Never believe anyone who tells you that an investment is sure to go up. If it is sure to go up, there would be no risk – and without risk, there can be no significant returns.

Currency speculation is a particularly risky form of investment, because it is difficult to predict the movements of any currency, even established ones. Given the volatility of the Iraqi economy, we would not place much confidence in the prospects of its fledgling currency.

What makes you and your *kollel* buddies sure that the dinar will go up? How do you know that it will not be devalued to even less than its current value? And why are you so confident that the conflict in Iraq will be successfully resolved?

Even if Iraqi dinars were worth investing in at some point, you can be sure that by the time you heard about the prospect in your *kollel*, the market price for dinars would have already corrected itself to reflect the latest speculative excitement and the resulting demand.

"Buy the rumor, sell the news" is an old principle of investing. Basically, it means that you should only put your money into an investment before it makes the headlines, not when everyone else has already heard about it and bought in. The new Iraqi dinar has been around since 2003, and has long ceased to be the hot rumor; it is not even news anymore.

Furthermore, there is no real market for Iraqi dinars nowadays. It is therefore unlikely that you will be able to sell your dinars at a profit; you might not even be able to liquidate them at all. And because dinars are not a very commonly traded currency, you will have to pay high commissions and change fees when purchasing them. So you are basically guaranteed a loss the moment you get your hands on any dinars.

Putting your money into Iraqi dinars, or any other "can't lose" proposition, is not investing, but gambling. As such, it cannot even be considered part of your requisite *hishtadlus* for *parnassah*. You would do your friends a service by cautioning them against buying Iraqi dinars and explaining to them that there is no such thing as easy money.

Common sense would dictate that you keep your money far away from anything remotely related to Iraq, and spare yourself the pain of watching your money disappear. As for your friends who have already invested in Iraqi dinars, we hope that they lose enough money early on to discourage them from dabbling blindly in speculative investments ever again.

Having dealt with many clients who lost everything in the process of getting rich quick, Mesila strongly discourages people from investing their money without the help of an investment professional. An investment professional will assess your complete financial situation, determine the level of risk appropriate for you, and help you find the investments that are right for you.

Reprinted from *Your Money and Your Life: Mesila's Down-to-Earth, Torah-Based Strategies for Managing Your Finances*, by M. Heimowitz

STUDENT RESOURCE 9

THE MYTH OF GUARANTEED RETURNS

Question: *When I got married about a year ago, my parents and in-laws put together a nice sum of money for us to live on for several years, and suggested that I invest it. I found out about a very promising real estate project that offered 18% interest and had very wealthy, reliable guarantors offering their personal guarantee. I invested the money into that project, and for the first few months after I invested, I was able to pay my rent with the interest. Then a problem arose with the project, and for the past three months, I have not received any interest payments. I have requested that my capital be returned, but a few weeks have passed and I have not received any money back.*

I recently heard about another real estate project that pays only 16% interest, but will give me a lien on the property as a guarantee. When I get my capital back, I hope to invest in this project, but in the meantime, I need money to pay my rent. Would it be advisable for me to borrow money to invest in this second project, in view of the fact that I have a solid guarantee to borrow against? One other question – at what point would it be appropriate for me to approach the guarantors of the first project?

A: Your situation is reminiscent of Chazal's saying, "*Mi she'achal shum, yachzor v'yochal shum?*" – if someone ate garlic (and is suffering from bad breath), should he go and eat more garlic? (*Shabbos* 31b).

You were burned once with a real estate investment that sounded, and was, too good to be true. Even if you had more of your own money to invest, why would you take a chance of getting burned again?

As a rule, you should be wary of any investment that offers returns higher than those paid by the bank. (Government bonds are the notable exception; they pay more than the bank, but are generally considered a safe investment.)

Phrases like "guaranteed returns" and "no risk" so often dupe novice investors into naively believing that they can invest their money, and voila, their financial worries will be over. At Mesila, we see the devastating results of this naïveté time and time again.

Although we do not know the details of either of the projects you describe, we can safely assume that any investments that promise such high returns are too risky. This assumption is based on the premise that anyone looking for investment capital would prefer to borrow at bank lending rates than at 16-18%. If a real estate project is offering returns of 16% on your money, you can be sure that no bank was willing to sink money into the project. Is your tolerance for risk, or risk appetite, greater than the bank's? Considering the fact that you do not have money to pay your rent, we think not.

In our opinion, it would be unconscionable for anyone to borrow money to invest in an enterprise as risky as the projects you have described. The lien you have been offered on the second property does not guarantee anything; if the property would be enough of a loan guarantee, the bank would have been very willing to take it as collateral, and there would have been no need for private investors like yourself. Do not let the offer of the lien blind you into risking more capital, especially if the money is borrowed. If you lose the capital – and with such high risk, there is a good chance that you *will* lose the capital – how will you repay the loan?

The money you invested in the first project is not money you can count on, and definitely not money you can borrow against. While we certainly hope that you will get back your money, you should be prepared for the possibility that it may take years of wrangling and legal action before you see a penny of it.

In answer to your second question, we recommend that you approach the guarantors of the first project immediately, before they are inundated with demands from other creditors. The fact that these guarantors were once wealthy and reliable is no assurance that they will be able to bear the financial backlash of a failed real estate proposition. You should therefore make sure that you are one of the first in line to receive any money that might be forthcoming.

As a final note, we wish to stress that risking capital for the promise of high returns is not only unwise from an investment standpoint, but is problematic from a Torah perspective as well. Yaakov Avinu went back across the Yabok River to retrieve some small jugs, the Midrash tells us, because *tzaddikim* value their money. The *sefer Be'er Yosef* explains that the reason *tzaddikim* value their money is not because they ascribe importance to material acquisition; rather, it is because they understand that everything they own is a gift from Hashem, and if Hashem gives a person something, he has an obligation to take care of it and use it properly.

When people put money into risky investments, it shows a certain disregard for the *hashgachah pratis* that decreed that the money should be theirs.

In your case, the capital you invested, and now wish to re-invest, is the hard-earned money given to you by your loving parents and in-laws. *Hakaras hatov* would dictate that you should be exceedingly careful not to squander this money.

When you do get back your capital, we urge you to seek the advice of a licensed financial advisor before you invest it again.

STUDENT RESOURCE 10

SAVINGS: THE LONG AND SHORT OF IT

Question: *I earn a respectable income, and I am B"H able to support my family adequately. We live relatively simply, and I don't think that we waste money on unnecessary purchases. The problem is that we can't seem to put anything aside for the future. Besides for our mortgage, we are not in debt, but we have no savings to speak of and we never have any extra money to put away for savings. This worries me tremendously. I know that financial experts say that people should save up for retirement and other future needs, and I would love to follow this advice, but frankly, saving money just seems like an impossible goal. Do you have any ideas for me?*

A: The first step towards successfully saving for the future is having an appreciation for the value and importance of savings. Your concern over your present inability to save is a clear indication that you do possess this appreciation, and we therefore think that a bit of guidance is all you need in order to begin saving.

Saving for the future makes sense financially, but it is not only financial experts who advocate saving for the future. The Maharsha states in his *Chiddushei Aggados* (*Niddah* 65b) that a person should put aside money for his old age. In his Responsa *Shevet Halevi* (4:1), Harav Shmuel Wosner *shlita* writes, "It is obvious that [for] something that is the nature of the world, such as old age or marrying off children… it is a mitzvah to prepare in advance so that he will not become dependent on others."

Clearly, then, it is incumbent upon every Jewish family to plan for their financial future and save up money to cover future needs.

How to Start Saving

Like you, many people tell Mesila that they are barely managing financially – or not managing at all – and that they cannot even begin to think about saving. But saving is not something you do when you have extra money. There *is* no such thing as "extra" money – no matter how much money a person has, there are always demands made on that money.

Saving is simply a habit. It is a habit that for some people comes naturally, and for others has to be learned. How do you get into the habit of savings? Here are some pointers for getting started:

› **Start small**. Put aside your pocket change at the end of the day, put aside $10 a week, or put aside 5% of your monthly paycheck – just save something. *Prutah prutah mitztarefes* – if you save consistently, the amounts will eventually add up. More important, saving small amounts regularly will get you into the habit of saving in a way that is almost painless.

› **Save now**. You will always have good reasons not to save. Don't let these good reasons stop you from putting away at least something. (A caveat to this pointer – if you are carrying high-interest debt – credit card debt, for instance – your priority should be debt repayment, and not savings. A balance on your credit card might cost you 18% interest – and that's a lot more than you'll earn on most savings plans or investments.)

- **Save your windfalls.** Any time unexpected money comes your way – in the form of product rebates, tax refunds, gifts, etc. – put at least a portion of it towards savings immediately.
- **Make savings automatic.** You can set up a savings plan that will withdraw a certain amount of money from your bank account every month, or you can arrange for a portion of your paycheck to go directly to savings. This way, you barely feel the pinch.
- **Save first.** The first expense that comes off your paycheck should be your savings. Too many people say that they will save what is left at the end of the month. Those are the people who never manage to save anything.
- **Make it a team effort.** Both husband and wife – and possibly children as well, depending on their ages – need to be actively involved in the savings habit in order for it to work.
- **Watch where the money goes.** People who keep track of where their money goes end up spending less and saving more. Knowing how you are spending your money gives you more control over your expenditures and helps you to make better spending decisions. This leaves you with more money to save. It also gives you the freedom to decide how to use your money, rather than allowing spending pressures to dictate where your money goes.

Once you have decided to start saving, the next step is to decide what to do with your savings. There are two important categories of savings: short-term and long-term. Each of these requires a different strategy.

Short-Term Savings

This is the money you'll need for emergencies and for foreseeable large expenses.

Everyone needs some short-term savings. If you don't have any short-term savings, even minor financial setbacks can have disastrous results. A burst pipe, or even something as predictable as summer camp, can land you in debt or force you to sell or forfeit some of your assets. You would not want to lose your house or your car because you are temporarily unable to make the payments.

Short-term savings can earn enough interest to keep up with inflation, but will never yield the high returns associated with higher-risk investments. When choosing a home for your short-term savings, your primary considerations should be accessibility, liquidity and safety of principal.

Where should you keep your short-term savings? In a place that is accessible enough to dip into in a time of real need yet not accessible enough to spend any time you run out of cash. We recommend that you put short-term savings in a separate bank account, in a trustworthy *gemach*, or in very low-risk investments such as money market accounts, money market funds, certificates of deposit, high-interest savings accounts (available at certain banks and financial institutions) or treasury bonds. Each of these options has its pros and cons, but all of them are relatively safe, relatively liquid (easy to convert to cash), and earn relatively low interest.

Your should *not* put your short-term savings in higher-risk investments such as stocks, commodities or real estate.

How much money should you keep in short-term savings? That depends on your situation and your family's needs. Financial professionals usually recommend setting aside at least three months' worth of living expenses to tide you over in the event of an emergency or temporary unemployment or disability.

Besides for this emergency fund, you should also save for expenses looming on the horizon: your annual car insurance bill, the sputtering refrigerator that will need to be replaced soon, your son's bar mitzvah, and so on. These expenses are all predictable, and you have two choices how to pay for them: save up money and *earn* interest, or borrow the money and *pay* interest (at a much higher rate).

Long-Term Savings

Long-term savings is the money you'll need for times of considerable financial strain, such as marrying off children and old age.

When choosing a home for your long-term savings, remember that inflation reduces the value of your money by about 3% a year. By keeping your long-term savings under your mattress, you actually lose money. It is therefore important to put your money in a place where it will earn respectable returns. That is why the term "investing" is used much more with regard to long-term savings than with regard to short-term savings.

With long-term savings, you have the opportunity to let your investments earn compound interest (interest on interest), which effortlessly multiplies your investment. But compound interest needs time to work its magic.

To illustrate: If you save $2,000 a year for 40 years (a total savings of $80,000) and earn interest of 8% annually, you will have $559,562 by the time you are finished. If you save $2,000 a year for 30 years (a total savings of $60,000) at the same interest rate of 8%, you will end up with $244,692 – less than half. (For comparison's sake, saving the same amount at an interest rate of 5% would give you $253,680 after 40 years and $139,522 after 30 years.)

Here's another example. Let's say you want to save about $50,000 for your son's wedding. If your son is a newborn, you need to save $100 a month at 8% for 18 years (a total savings of $21,600) to have that amount. If your son is 13, you will need to save $430 a month for 7 years at 8% (a total savings of $36,120) to have that same $50,000 by the time he turns 20.

People in their 20s don't usually think much about marrying off their children or about their retirement, but if they would, they would reap the rewards later. When you are young, you can invest relatively little and wind up with far more money than someone older who saves much more.

The simplest way to start saving for retirement is to sign up for your employer's pension plan (known as a 401(k) in the U.S.). If this is not an option, you should speak to a financial adviser about starting your own tax-deferred savings plan (known as an IRA in the U.S.). People in Israel should speak to an insurance agent who specializes in pension planning.

Putting money into stocks and stock funds – a terrible idea for short-term savings – is actually a very good idea for long-term savings. The stock market is notorious for its volatility, but over the past 80 years it has yielded an average return of about 10% – higher than any other type of investment.

Another advantage of the stock market is that you have the option of investing even minimal amounts. Even if you cannot afford to put away a lot of money, you can still enjoy the long-term benefits of stock market investments.

Higher returns like those associated with the stock market usually involve higher risks. When you are investing for the long term, however, you are able to accept more risk. Since time is on your side, you have the ability to ride out the ups and downs of the economy without being affected every time the market takes a hit.

When investing in the stock market, we strongly discourage active investing or day trading. The approach we advocate is "buy and hold," in which you allow your portfolio to grow over time without selling or exchanging specific investments.

To minimize your risks, it is important to maintain a diversified investment portfolio. This is in keeping with Chazal's advice (*Bava Metzia* 42b) to keep a third of your assets in real estate, a third in merchandise, and a third liquid.

Diversification ensures that your financial future is not dependent on the performance of any one investment. Mutual funds (including index funds and retirement funds) are a common type of diversified investment, although not all mutual funds are created equal.

A good investment portfolio contains a mixture of stocks, bonds and real estate investments. The exact mixture should be determined based on your level of risk tolerance, which depends on factors such as your present financial situation, your future financial goals, and the age and number of your dependents. We recommend that you work with a licensed financial advisor to decide what types of investments are appropriate for you.

As you approach the time when you are going to need to withdraw money from long-term savings, financial experts recommend that you shift some of your holdings into bonds, which are considered less profitable but also less volatile than stocks. In this way, you are protected if the stock market suddenly crashes just before you need to dip into your savings.

In comparison to stocks and bonds, certain real estate and business investments require a much larger initial outlay and a far more sophisticated investment strategy. Novice investors should steer clear of these types of investments, which necessitate professional evaluation, extensive research, a thorough understanding of the market, and a high level of risk tolerance.

Once you have started a long-term savings plan, stick with it. There will always be new investment possibilities on the horizon that sound more exciting and promise higher returns, but in the end, the simple, steady and boring usually outperforms the new, exciting and lucrative.

It's never too late – or too early – to start saving for the future. The key is to determine what your savings goals are, and to start – today!

Reprinted from *Your Money and Your Life: Mesila's Down-to-Earth, Torah-Based Strategies for Managing Your Finances*, by M. Heimowitz

STUDENT RESOURCE 11

THE MAGIC OF COMPOUND INTEREST
OR
THE TIME VALUE OF MONEY

Once upon a time, Meir and Shneur were 12-year-old twin brothers who sold a lot of lemonade in their spare time. Their grandmother promised to match any money they saved up in an IRA (IRA: A personal retirement plan that enjoys special tax benefits), which was paying 7.5% compound interest (don't forget, this is a fairy tale).

Meir managed to put aside $600 a year, which his grandmother matched, for a total of $1200, and they continued this arrangement for 10 years.

Shneur, in the meantime, bought a lot of rebbe cards. When he decided to stop collecting 10 years later, at age 22, he found himself with some extra cash, and he too began to take advantage of Bubby's largesse. He opened his own IRA and put away $1200 for the next 24 years, until Bubby passed away.

At that point, Meir and Shneur decided to take a peek at their accounts and see how much money was in there.

Table A

At age	Meir saves	Shneur saves
12	$1200	$0
13	$1200	$0
14	$1200	$0
15	$1200	$0
16	$1200	$0
17	$1200	$0
18	$1200	$0
19	$1200	$0
20	$1200	$0
21	$1200	$0

Table B

At age	If Meir stops saving	If Meir continues saving	Shneur starts saving
22	$0	$1200	$1200
23	$0	$1200	$1200
24	$0	$1200	$1200
25	$0	$1200	$1200
26	$0	$1200	$1200
27	$0	$1200	$1200
28	$0	$1200	$1200
29	$0	$1200	$1200
30	$0	$1200	$1200
31	$0	$1200	$1200
32	$0	$1200	$1200
33	$0	$1200	$1200
34	$0	$1200	$1200
35	$0	$1200	$1200
36	$0	$1200	$1200
37	$0	$1200	$1200
38	$0	$1200	$1200
39	$0	$1200	$1200
40	$0	$1200	$1200
41	$0	$1200	$1200
42	$0	$1200	$1200
43	$0	$1200	$1200
44	$0	$1200	$1200
45	$0	$1200	$1200
Total IRA contribution:	$12,000	$40,000	$28,000
Total account value:	**$96,307**	**$169,872**	**$73,566**

Look at what happened:

Meir's contribution in the first 10 years, totaling $12,000, grows to $96,307 by age 45 – even if he stops contributing at age 21. Shneur, who begins investing at age 22, contributes a total of $28,000 over 24 years, but his account value at age 45 is still less than Meir's. Shneur contributed more than twice as much money but still hasn't caught up with Meir – all because he procrastinated. The story of Meir and Shneur illustrates the magic of compounding interest, or the time value of money.

Our example uses an IRA as a savings plan, but the principle is true regardless of what type of investment account you have. The moral of the story: Start saving *now*.

STUDENT RESOURCE 12

PAYMENT METHODS

CASH

Pros

- People know whether they have money to spend.
- The money is tangible, not an abstract number on a bank or credit card statement. This creates greater psychological resistance to parting with it, and leads people to think more about spending it.
- From the standpoint of financial responsibility and restraint, many of the disadvantages of cash are actually advantages.

Cons

- People often don't have cash readily available, and obtaining cash can be a hassle.
- Obtaining cash may involve bank fees.
- There is no recourse in the event of loss or theft.
- Once payment is made, the money cannot be retrieved. (Unlike a check or credit card payment that can be stopped.)
- Payment has to be made in person; it cannot be made by telephone, by mail or online.
- Cash transactions are difficult to track or keep records of.
- Possibility of counterfeit bills.

CHECK

Pros

- Payment can be made by mail.
- Can be used when there is no cash available.
- Can be post-dated to delay payment.
- Can be stopped in the event of loss, theft, or a payment dispute.
- Convenient as a deposit on a purchase or as a form of guarantee.
- Payment can be made in advance, on any date in the future.

Cons

- Check payments are difficult to track because it is uncertain when the checks will be deposited.
- When more than one person is writing checks on an account, it can lead to chaos.
- Bounced checks, or checks that have mistakes or other technical problems can lead to inconvenience, embarrassment and hefty charges.
- Possibility of fraud.
- Ease of delaying payment may cause people to go into debt.

CREDIT CARD

Pros

- Convenient and available.
- Insurance against theft.
- Easy to cancel in the event of loss.
- Payment can be made by telephone or online.
- Can be used anywhere in the world.
- Can be used by all members of the family.
- Easy to track.
- Credit limits make it impossible to spend more than a certain amount.
- Payment can be made in installments.
- Earn air miles and rewards.

Cons

- People spend more (30% more, studies show) because it is convenient and because they do not feel the pain of parting with their money.
- Multiple credit cards can lead to chaos.
- Paying in installments can lead to exceeding budgetary limits.
- Credit option can be halachically problematic.
- Credit cards deceive people into thinking that they have money when they really do not.
- Incurs high interest if paid late.

STUDENT RESOURCE 13

DR. SEUSS ON Consumerism

Consumerism is based on creating needs where none existed before.

In **The Lorax**, by Dr. Seuss, a fellow opens a factory for a new type of garment called a "Thneed," and a creature named the Lorax ridicules him for creating this useless item. To which the fellow responds:

"A Thneed's a fine something that all people need!
It's a shirt. It's a sock. It's a glove. It's a hat.
But it has other uses. Yes, far beyond that.
You can use it for carpets. For pillows! For sheets!
Or curtains! Or covers for bicycle seats!"

The Lorax said, "Sir! You are crazy with greed.
There is no one on earth
who would buy that fool Thneed!"
But the very next minute I proved he was wrong.
For, just at that minute, a chap came along,
and he thought that the Thneed I had knitted was great.
He happily bought it for three ninety-eight.

I laughed at the Lorax, "You poor stupid guy!
You never can tell what some people will buy."

STUDENT RESOURCE 14

AM I A SHOPAHOLIC?

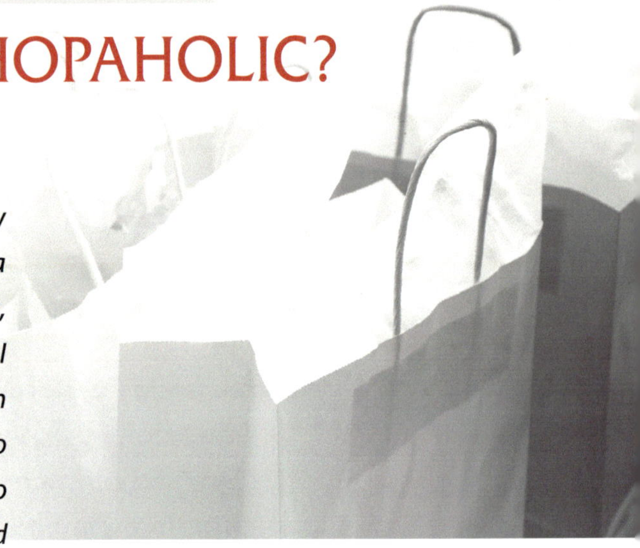

Question: *Shopping has been my favorite pastime ever since I've been a teenager. I love to buy things – groceries, clothing, household items, you name it. I often find myself heading out to a store in the evenings when I have nothing else to do. I've noticed a pattern in which I'll go into a store on the spur of the moment and buy a few things, only to go back to that store a few days later to return some items, at which point I'll inevitably find something else to purchase. My family members and friends comment about my spending habits, calling me a "shopaholic" and telling me that I spend too much. How do I know if I really have a spending problem? And if I do have a spending problem, how can I overcome it?*

A: Not knowing the details of your lifestyle and spending habits, we cannot tell you whether you have a spending problem. But we can tell you that your willingness to confront the issue is a very good first step in overcoming your spending problem, if indeed you have one.

When does spending become a problem? Any type of behavior or characteristic taken to an extreme is problematic, and spending is no different. The Rambam teaches us that the middle road is the golden path, and the ability to strike a balance between the two extremes in every middah is the hallmark of healthy behavior.

Spending problems come in two varieties – stinginess and extravagance, representing the two polar extremes of the spending spectrum. Our goal is to find a middle road that allows us to spend enough to meet our needs and obligations, but not so much that we squander money needlessly.

The terms "stinginess" and "extravagance" are quite subjective, because the size of a person's budget is a major factor in determining whether the person spends too much or too little. But how much money a person has is by no means the only factor in determining whether he or she has a spending problem. Spending problems are as a much a behavioral issue as a financial issue. There are poor people who are miserly, and there are rich people who are miserly. There are poor people who overspend, and there are rich people who overspend.

The sign of a stinginess problem is when a person has difficulty spending money on items that he and his family clearly require – not because he doesn't have the money, but because he cannot bring himself to spend it. This creates an atmosphere of deprivation and penny-

Reprinted from *Your Money and Your Life: Mesila's Down-to-Earth, Torah-Based Strategies for Managing Your Finances*, by M. Heimowitz

pinching in the home, which is often accompanied by a fixation with money and prices.

When does overspending become a problem? For every person, the line between healthy spending and overspending will be drawn in a different place, but we can identify four general parameters that can help you to determine whether you are overspending.

1. **You spend more than you can afford.** There are three ways to assess whether you are spending more than you can afford. One, if you consistently spend more than you earn, and you either accumulate debt or eat away at your savings as a result. Two, if your income is reasonable but you are nevertheless unable to put aside any money for the future. And three, if you spend money on luxury or non-essential items and you are then unable to pay for basic or essential items.

2. **You spend money to fill an emotional void.** While shopping can be a pleasurable experience and can provide some measure of stress relief, it should not be used consistently as an outlet for negative feelings such as sadness, inadequacy, boredom, guilt, fear, anger, or nervousness. Spending money is not a healthy response to negative feelings, because the act of swiping a credit card and walking away with a shopping bag does nothing to dispel the source of those feelings. Any feeling of emotional relief that shopping provides is therefore short-lived and superficial.

3. **You buy things that you do not need and never use.** If your closet is full of items that still have price tags, if you often wonder what possessed you to buy a particular item that you have no use for, or if you frequently make excuses for – or worse, lie about – your purchases and how much they cost, then it is likely that your spending is problematic.

4. **Your spending is adversely affecting other areas of your life.** Even if you and your family are not suffering financially because of your spending habits, your spending might be harmful to you or to your loved ones in other ways. Do you have frequent arguments with your family members about your spending habits? Are your children being neglected because you are out shopping too much? Has your marriage been reduced to a collection of shared things, instead of shared goals and shared communication? Does your life revolve around material acquisition, to the point that you are desensitized to the pleasures of spirituality and meaningful relationships?

Severe Overspending

In extreme cases, people can actually develop an addiction to shopping – known scientifically as oniomania, or colloquially as "shopaholism" – if they get used to spending money in order to squelch negative feelings. These people might buy ten items when they really need only one, or they might pay outrageous amounts of money for things they have little or no use for.

Shopping addicts experience a rush of endorphins when they spend money, which gives them a brief but exhilarating escape from life's painful realities. As soon as that feeling of euphoria subsides, they begin to crave the pleasurable sensation they associate with shopping, and they feel an uncontrollable urge to spend money again. Between spending episodes, shopping addicts are typically plagued by anxiety, shame, and guilt, and think about money excessively. This cycle is typical of addictive behavior, and professional intervention is usually required in order to break the cycle.

Overcoming the Problem

If your spending has reached out-of-control proportions, to the point where it can be classified as compulsive or addictive, then you will need to seek professional help. But if you still have some measure of control over your spending, we will offer several suggestions for reining it in to a point where it is no longer problematic.

› Don't carry your wallet with you when you don't need it. If you don't have money or a credit card with you, then you will have to come back later if you want to buy an item that you see. This is a good way to test whether you really need or want the item, and can help to reduce impulse purchases.

› Get rid of your credit cards. When used properly, credit cards can be a very convenient and useful tool. But if you have a tendency to overspend, you should avoid credit cards completely. Credit cards make it dangerously easy to spend money, since they eliminate the pain you experience when you have to part with your money. The pain of parting with money is actually a healthy pain, because it ensures that you item you are spending money on justifies the pain involved.

› Shop when you are not sad, stressed, excited, or in a rush. People tend to spend more, and buy things they don't need, when they are feeling down, or when they are under pressure. People who are very happy, excited, or on an emotional high also tend to spend more. And the less time people have, the more money they tend to spend.

› Avoid temptation. Stay away from the stores you tend to spend money in. If you have a particular friend who spends a lot, don't go shopping with her.

› Develop constructive emotional outlets. There are many constructive ways to relieve negative feelings, but spending money is not one of them. If you are feeling down, talk to a friend, pick up a Tehillim, or go for a walk, instead of heading instinctively for the mall. Keep in mind that "retail therapy" is therapeutic for retailers, not for customers.

› Find alternative recreational activities. You don't have to buy anything in order to have a good time. Instead of associating shopping with leisure and relaxation, condition yourself to see shopping primarily as a functional and task-oriented activity, and plan leisure activities that do not involve any purchases.

› Learn to express love and gratitude in non-tangible ways. People who enjoy buying things often ascribe disproportionate value or importance to tangible objects and resort to gift-giving in order to express love and gratitude. But emotions like these are best expressed in words, whether spoken or written. Tangible gifts should be reserved for special occasions; otherwise, they lose their value in the eye of the recipient. Even when you do decide to buy a gift, remember that a gift is only as meaningful as the sentiment underlying it, and the amount of money you spend on a gift does not determine its value.

› Build a budget that includes an allowance for discretionary spending. If you tend to overspend, then it is doubly important for you to have a clearly defined budget that governs the amount you spend on variable expenditures such as food, clothing, gifts, and household items. But in order for you to succeed in sticking to your budget, it is also important that you give yourself some breathing room and allocate some money towards non-essential or impulse purchases. This way, you will not feel stifled by your budget and you will not be tempted to abandon it any time you succumb to the temptation to buy something that is not absolutely necessary. To make sure that you remain accountable to your budget, you should build it together with your spouse or a close friend or relative, and review it together with that person on a regular basis.

We welcome readers' suggestions for other ways to kick the overspending habit, and we wish you much hatzlachah.

STUDENT RESOURCE 15

CREDIT CARD SCENARIOS

Please, Please - Don't Let This be You!

What can be done to help these people ?

Situation #1

I am 28 years old and I am married with 4 kids. Over the past few years our expenses amounted to more then we could afford and we used credit cards to cover the difference. Currently my wife and I owe $20,000 in credit card debt and $15,000 in private debt. All our credit cards are maxed out, we are unable to make the monthly payments of roughly $1,400, and we are struggling to pay our living expenses. I believe that the money we have coming in is enough – or even slightly more than enough – for us to live on, but we can't get out of the credit card debt cycle. The situation has proven to be overwhelming for my family and we desperately need help in getting out of debt and figuring out how to stay out of it in the future.

Situation #2

My husband is learning in Lakewood, and I have a very good job that should bring in enough to support us and our six kids. I'm very careful with what I spend but somehow every month I find myself putting a small amount on the credit card. It's usually children's clothes on sale, special food for Yom Tov, or small household items that I pick up here and there. It doesn't seem like a lot, but I was shocked to realize that recently, my credit card balance ballooned to upwards of $30,000! This was all in interest and late charges that accrued because I was not careful to make my minimum payments and my credit rating deteriorated to the point that my interest rates went up tremendously. My husband and I are considering selling our house and moving out of town where my husband can join an out of town kollel in order to pay off the debt. It would be difficult to leave my home and the town that I love. Does Mesila think this is the right step to take?

Situation #3

My husband is in chinuch and we've always lived very simply. When we married off our oldest daughter we discovered credit cards. We had some savings, but we wanted our new kallah to be happy, and there were more expenses to deal with than we ever imagined so before we knew it, we had $50,000 in credit card, no credit rating to speak of, and we could barely afford to pay off the interest that was accruing rapidly from month to month. The principal has remained the same for eight years (but our son-in-law's value has grown!). What should we do?

Situation #4

I'm a successful businessman and my wife takes care of running all aspects of the household – including shopping, unfortunately. How she manages to spend thousands of dollars each month on clothing and trinkets is beyond me, but the credit card bill doesn't lie. One swipe, lots of packages, and another $800 is gone. When I ask her about it, she just says, "Well, we can afford it, can't we?" or, "It was on sale, it was a great deal, how could I leave it in the store?" or "We really needed this." If she wouldn't have the credit card, I don't think she'd be spending half as much. She thinks we can afford it, but there's a limit to how much I earn and I'd really like to save money for other, more important things. Besides, I'm finding myself feeling stressed at the end of the month many times.

STUDENT RESOURCE 16

CLIMBING THE MOUNTAIN OF CREDIT CARD DEBT

Question: *I know that Mesila is against using credit cards, but I have found that it is difficult for me to keep the right amounts of cash on hand, and I often resort to using my credit card. As a result, I've built up a bit of a balance on my credit card – or cards, I should say – and I'm wondering if you have any advice how I can pay it off.*

A: Mesila is not, in principle, opposed to credit cards, nor do we consider cash the preferred payment method in all situations. One of Mesila's guiding principles is to promote financial management principles and attitudes that are universally relevant, while avoiding specific tips and suggestions. So rather than issuing a blanket statement regarding whether you should be using credit cards or not, we will share several general guidelines that should help you decide for yourself.

Credit cards can be a very useful and convenient tool, when used correctly. The trouble is that many people misuse their credit cards by charging more than they can afford each month. Credit card companies actually *rely* on people misusing their cards; in fact, interest charged on outstanding balances represents the primary way in which credit card companies generate revenue. In 2007, people in the U.S. who carried a monthly balance paid $18.1 billion in penalty fees. With annual earnings of about $30 billion, the credit card industry is the most profitable one in the United States.

There are many advantages to using credit cards. You never run of out money. You are generally insured against theft, and you can easily cancel the card if you lose it. In contrast, cash that is lost or stolen is usually gone forever. You can use your credit card to pay for purchases by telephone or online, rather than mailing a check or paying by cash in person. Most credit cards can be used anywhere in the world, regardless of the local currency, and you can order cards for all of your family members. Depending on the card issuer's policy, purchases made using the card may be protected against theft, loss, or accidental damage that occurs within a certain period of time.

Credit card statements make it relatively straightforward to track your purchases on a monthly basis and keep a record of how your money is being spent. Cash, on the other hand, has no paper trail, and it is difficult to remember exactly where the money in your wallet went.

We will point out that all of these advantages are available through bank or debit cards as well, although purchase protection may not be offered on certain debit cards. The big difference, however, is that these cards draw on money that is already in your bank account, rather than creating a de facto debt that has to be paid at the end of the billing cycle. The only feature that credit cards offer that debit cards do not usually have is the possibility of earning rewards, in the form of airline miles, cash-back offers, or other perks.

So much for the advantages of using credit cards. Now let's talk about the drawbacks. Drawback number one is that they make it deceptively easy to spend money, whether you have the money or you don't. The act of swiping a credit card is not nearly as painful as taking actual money out of your wallet, and the psychological deterrent to parting with your money is therefore lessened considerably when paying with a credit card. Studies show that people spend about 30% more when paying by credit card than when paying with cash, and we think it is fair to assume that the extra 30% is money that could have been put to better use.

The other major drawback of credit cards is that they are a form of loan. When you take a loan, you borrow money and commit to repaying it at a later date. When you use a credit card, you also borrow money – but without realizing it. Mesila's philosophy is that a loan in which you realize that you are borrowing money is preferable to a loan in which you do not realize that you are borrowing money, simply because you are less likely to borrow, and more likely to repay, when the decision to take the loan was a conscious one.

Credit card debt is one of the worst forms of debt, for two reasons. One, it usually carries very high interest rates. Two, there is no repayment deadline for the debt. As long as you keep making minimum payments, credit card companies are quite happy to keep tacking interest onto your balance and let your debt swell to ever-greater proportions. Unpleasant as it may be to have creditors breathing down your back, it is a far healthier situation when a debt is collected at the end of its term than when a debt is allowed to balloon endlessly.

Not only do credit cards charge high interest rates, but there is very little limit as to how much they can raise your rate. Credit card companies are legally allowed to monitor your credit report, and should you make a late payment on a loan, a different credit card, or a utility bill, your interest rates can be increased dramatically, even if you have never missed a payment on that particular card. There are a number of other reasons you may see your rates spike. These include bouncing a check, exceeding your credit limit, having too much debt or credit, getting a new credit card, and applying for an auto loan or mortgage.

Because credit card debt is so dangerous, our advice is that the only people who should use credit cards are those who (a) can rein in their spending despite the painless convenience of plastic and (b) pay their balance in full every month consistently. People who swipe their cards without giving it the same thought that they would when spending cash should rather spend cash, unless they are paying for something that they cannot possibly be spending more for by using a credit card (dental work, for instance, or a utility bill). And people who carry over a balance on their credit cards, even occasionally, should probably avoid using credit cards completely.

If you are able to use a credit card correctly, there are a few things we recommend:

› *Choose the right card.*

Make sure that your card provides a grace period of at least 20 days from the date of purchase until payment is due. Without a grace period, you'll be charged interest before you even get your bill. There are cards that offer airline miles, cash back on purchases, and points for rewards programs, and if you are using a credit card, you might as well get something in return. However, if there is an annual fee associated with your rewards card, make sure the benefits outweigh the cost.

› *Don't have too many cards.*

Keeping track of even one credit card can be quite a challenge. When keeping track of two or more cards, mistakes (such as missed payments or forgetting to cancel the card before annual fees kick in) are more likely to go by unnoticed. Unless you have a very good reason for keeping a second or third credit card, get rid of it.

But what if you have already fallen into credit card debt? Here are some suggestions for climbing out of the morass.

› *Ask for clemency.*

If you missed only one payment, you can call your credit card company and ask them to waive interest and late fees. Credit card companies will waive these fees on occasion, if you generally pay on time.

› *Stop using your credit cards.*

If you're already behind on your monthly payments, don't aggravate the situation by accumulating more credit card debt. Although this may seem obvious, it is actually the opposite of how people generally work. The tendency is that once people owe money, they lose a major psychological deterrent towards borrowing, and they let their debt slowly inflate. ("What's the difference if I owe $600 or $900?" "If I already owe $60,000, another $5,000 won't make any difference.") Cut your losses *now*, and don't allow yourself to charge even one additional item.

› *Take out a loan to pay off your credit card debt.*

Almost any type of loan is preferable to credit card debt because interest rates are generally much lower and there is a specific repayment timeframe. With a loan, you can work out repayment terms that reflect your ability to repay, which helps you discipline yourself to put aside a fixed sum every month for debt repayment. With credit card debt, there is no such discipline, since there is no obligation to repay anything more than the minimum payment.

› *Do a balance transfer to another card.*

While you will pay a fee, transferring your outstanding balance to a card with a lower interest rate will decrease the amount you carry from month to month. By doing a balance transfer instead of allowing interest fees to build up, you give yourself some breathing room to pay off your debt. But beware – this is a very stopgap measure. You can't keep doing balance transfers for very long since there are only so many transfers credit card companies will allow you to do, and besides, multiple balance transfers will cause your finances to become chaotic.

› *Find a card with a low interest rate.*

Some credit cards offer relatively low interest rates. Shopping around for a better rate than the one you currently have can save you hundreds or even thousands of dollars a month (that is, if your credit rating is good enough for you to be eligible for these offers). Look out, however, for introductory offers that end after several months or exclusions that limit the low rate to new purchases only.

› *Negotiate a better interest rate.*

You might have to spend a long time on the phone with your credit card company, but it's worth it to get your interest rate reduced by even a few points. If possible, ask your company to match another company's offer. If your company is unwilling to cooperate, you can mention that you may be forced to declare personal bankruptcy, if that is really an option. This gets the companies scared, because they are the ones who stand to lose from a bankruptcy.

› *Never, ever miss a minimum payment.*

Missing minimum payments is a big no-no, and can severely damage your credit rating. Having a good credit rating is important, because many types of creditors besides credit card companies – including utilities, hospitals, landlords, insurance companies, and banks – can report delinquent payments to credit bureaus, as well as access your credit history. Since credit card companies are among those monitoring and contributing to customers' credit reports, a late or missed payment on one charge account could cause your rates and fees to increase on a completely separate account – even your car insurance premiums.

Pay off credit card balances from smallest to largest.

The smallest debts are the easiest to

pay off, and clearing them out of the way helps you make the fastest progress towards getting your finances in order. The fewer debts you have to pay back, the easier it will be to see the light at the end of the tunnel, and the more motivated you will be to tackle the larger, scarier debts.

› ***Make micro-payments.***

In addition to the minimum payments, send in whatever small amounts you can to gradually pay off your balance.

› ***Get professional debt counseling assistance.***

Climbing a mountain of credit card debt can be a very tough task to tackle alone. If there is a Mesila branch in your community, we encourage you to apply for our family counseling program. If there is no Mesila branch in your community, seek the guidance of a qualified debt counselor.

STUDENT RESOURCE 17

TRADING SECURITIES

LifeLines › C. Saphir

Trading Securities

When you're an American living in Israel, the Seudas Hamafsekes on Erev Yom Kippur is prime time for overseas phone calls. As you sit down to your meal, your loved ones seven hours behind are just starting their day, and calling to wish you a *gemar chasimah tovah* and maybe ask for *mechilah* for some forgotten misdeed.

68 MISHPACHA

In the midst of one such Seudas Hamafsekes, a very familiar number appeared on our phone's caller ID screen.

"Gavriel Klein?" I wondered aloud to my wife, Perri. "What could he possibly want? Not *mechilah*, obviously."

"Yitzi?" a familiar voice drawled. "I'm calling to ask you for *mechilah*."

WE HAD BEEN LIVING in Yerushalayim for about five years, scraping by in *kollel*, and we were starting to think about options for *parnassah*. Perri was working, and I was *shteiging*, but we were having a hard time "finishing the month." In that respect, we were no different from many other *frum* families in Israel, although we did draw the line at taking *gemach* loans; there was no way we'd go into debt to finance our regular living expenses.

What allowed us to sleep at night was the knowledge that we had some money safely stashed away in an IRA retirement fund. Shortly after our wedding, upon the advice of my financial advisor (aka my father-in-law), we had taken our nest egg and invested it in retirement savings. Not that we were planning to use those savings in the near future, of course, but having that cushion gave us the security of knowing that in an emergency, we'd have what to fall back on.

One of the nice things about living in Yerushalayim is that you get to give back to many of the people who helped you over the years, by hosting their children for Shabbos and Yom Tov. When I had learned in Israel as a *bochur*, I had often eaten meals at the home of a second cousin of mine named Gavriel Klein. My parents hadn't been too thrilled about my becoming a regular guest of Gavriel's — they seemed not to like him, for some inexplicable reason — but I felt very comfortable at his table, and since he was my only American relative in the country, his house naturally became a home away from home for me. Now, Gavriel's son Aharon was learning in Yerushalayim, and he started coming to us regularly for Shabbos.

Not only did we appreciate the opportunity to reciprocate Gavriel's kindness, we also enjoyed having Aharon over. He was a sweet, polite boy who entertained the kids, helped clear the table, and asked for seconds of whatever Perri served. A few times, I remarked to Perri that it was a shame our oldest daughter, Rivky, was too young to marry Aharon; I'd have had no compunctions about letting Rivky marry this third cousin of hers.

One day, Aharon called me to ask for a favor. "My father needs a big check cashed," he said. "It's a $15,000 check, and no moneychanger is willing to change it for me. They're saying they need someone to vouch for the check. Are you able to do that?"

"Sure," I said. I wondered why Gavriel needed to change such a big check, but I figured it wasn't really my business. After all that he had done for me when I was a *bochur*, the least I could do for him was sign for his check.

"There's a moneychanger named Leifer that I often use," I told Aharon. "He knows me, and I'm sure he'd be willing to take the check. Meet me there tomorrow afternoon."

Aharon met me at the moneychanger, I signed for the check, Leifer counted out $15,000 minus the change fee, and I forgot about the whole incident.

About a month later, I got a call from Leifer. "The check bounced," he informed me. "Call your friend in America and tell him I need a new check right away."

"I'm so sorry," I said, feeling quite embarrassed. "I'll take care of it, don't worry."

Immediately, I called Gavriel and told him what had happened. "I don't believe it!" Gavriel exclaimed. "There was one day a few weeks back when my balance dipped under $15,000, and they must have tried to deposit the check exactly on that day. What lousy timing! I'm really sorry about this, and I'll get another check over to Aharon as soon as I can."

It took three weeks for the new check to arrive, during which time Leifer became quite irritated, calling me every other day and declaring, *"Zeh lo b'seder. Zeh mamash lo b'seder."* I didn't want to pressure Gavriel, but the situation was really uncomfortable for me, and so when Aharon finally arrived at my door bearing a fresh check, I felt very relieved.

Two weeks after that, Leifer called again. "The check bounced again. *Lo b'seder! Mamash lo b'seder!* I need you to pay the $15,000 — now! Plus, I had all sorts of headaches and penalties with this check, and you owe me for all that, too."

I was shocked. How could Gavriel's second check have bounced? I tried calling him, but I didn't get through. I left an urgent message on his voicemail, and another urgent message with his wife, but I didn't hear back from him that day. When I finally got hold of him the next day, he apologized profusely, explaining that he was under a lot of financial pressure. "I had some unexpected expenses this month that emptied my account," he explained. "But I'm writing you another check as we speak. I'll have it for you by next week, the latest."

But Leifer wasn't willing to wait. "It's over two months since you gave me that first bad check," he said. "I need the money now, and I'm not waiting for another bad check to turn up."

My protestations that this time the check would be good didn't

The question was, now that this safety net had been yanked out from under us, HOW WAS I GOING TO REACT? Was I going to have trouble sleeping at night, worrying how I would cope with the expenses looming on the horizon? Or would I sleep soundly, with the serenity of a baby resting in its mother's arms?

make a dent in Leifer's insistence that I pay. As the sole guarantor on the check, I knew I was obligated to stand behind it. And so, having no alternative, I emptied our IRA account — which had almost exactly $15,000 in it — and used the money to pay Leifer.

The bank charged a hefty penalty for cashing in the retirement fund early. To cover that penalty, as well as the penalties Leifer passed on to me, I had to borrow money from a *gemach* — something I had never done in my life.

In the meantime, Perri and I were calling and e-mailing Gavriel frantically. "We just emptied our IRA and used up all of our savings to cover the check," I told Gavriel's voicemail countless times. "We need the money desperately! Please call back."

There was no response.

When I called Aharon to ask what was going on, he seemed completely befuddled. "I asked my father about it a few times, and he got very upset and told me it's none of my business," he reported. "I feel terrible, but I don't know what I can do."

I decided to discuss this predicament with my father-in-law — and regretted that decision almost immediately. "What?" he exclaimed. "You emptied your IRA? Don't you know that you never, ever touch your retirement savings? And why on earth would you vouch for someone else's check?"

I tried to explain that Gavriel wasn't just someone — I owed him tremendous *hakaras hatov*, and I trusted him implicitly. "I was practically a *ben bayis* in his house," I explained. "And he's my second cousin! How could I not do him the favor of signing his check?"

"I don't care who the guy is!" my father-in-law fumed. "You're a *kollel* guy, you shouldn't be getting involved in other people's financial stuff."

My parents were equally appalled — but not entirely surprised. "You vouched for Gavriel, of all people?" my father asked. "Don't you know he's Mr. Funny Money himself?"

"He is?" I asked in shock. "How was I supposed to know?"

"I warned you, when you were a *bochur*, to stay away from him. Since he's a kid, he's been up to all sorts of slippery money tricks. Why didn't you ask me before you signed his check?"

I felt like a fool.

Only Perri understood. "Of course we trusted Gavriel," she said soothingly. "Your parents never told us about his underhanded dealings, and even if they never liked him, the fact was that we had a longstanding relationship with him, and it was the most natural thing in the world for us to vouch for his check."

The way she said "we" and "us" — as though it wasn't only *my* fault — made me feel a thousand times better.

"Your father thinks I'm out of my mind for liquidating the IRA," I added.

"What's worse, stealing or emptying an IRA?" she asked rhetorically. "We signed for that check, and whether or not we were foolish for doing that, we're the ones who have to pay, now that Gavriel defaulted. The IRA isn't a holy cow — if that's the only money we had, that's what we had to use. We can second-guess ourselves from here to tomorrow, but I think we just need to accept that this was *min haShamayim*, and move on."

Eventually, calling from a different number, we managed to get Gavriel on the line. "Yes, I know, I have to send you a new check," he said calmly. "I just sold a property, and as soon as the money comes through, you'll have your check. It's just a matter of days."

We wanted to believe him. And we really did believe that he'd come through with the money at some point — after all, he couldn't, wouldn't, steal outright from his cousin and former *ben bayis*. Despite my parents' skepticism, Perri and I continued to hope that Gavriel's parade of excuses would end with an apology and a good check to back it up.

We kept calling him, every few days. Even when we realized that his assurances were meaningless, and he really wasn't planning to make good on the check, we didn't give up. How could we? That money was our cushion, our security blanket.

One day, as I was working out a schedule to repay my *gemach* loan, a thought occurred to me. *Do you really think an IRA is going to be your salvation, Yitzi? Never mind the fact that it was worth only $15,000 — even if it had been worth $150,000, or $15 million, was that what gave you security in life?*

In modern Hebrew, the word for security is "*bitachon*." A security guard is an "*ish bitachon*," whether or not he believes in a Higher Power. When you call the National Insurance Institute (Bituach Leumi), you hear the jingle, "Bituach Leumi, *habitachon sheli*." Had I, too, traded true *bitachon* for the illusory security of money in the bank?

Until that moment, I had viewed this experience as pure *agmas nefesh*. It was a *nisayon*, possibly a punishment, definitely something negative. All of a sudden, the whole sequence of events took on a different hue: Maybe this was Hashem's way of drawing us closer to Him, prodding us to rely *only* on Him and remove the supposed "security" that stood as a barrier to true *bitachon*.

I didn't regret having invested our money in an IRA — that was a legitimate *hishtadlus*, and one that I would have readily duplicated had I come across another windfall. The question was, now that this safety net had been yanked out from under us, how was I going to react? Was I going to have trouble sleeping at night, worrying how I would cope with the expenses looming on the horizon? Or would I sleep soundly, with the serenity of a baby resting in its mother's arms?

With or without the IRA, my time in *kollel* was drawing to a close, and it was time to start putting out feelers for possible employment opportunities. But my new realization about the meaning of *bitachon* cast this job search in a whole new light. This wasn't about looking for a job because my family would starve otherwise — it was about knowing that Hashem was providing for us, even as I sought to fulfill my duty to support my family. The difference was immense, and gauged not in terms of how much effort I'd invest into earning *parnassah*, but rather in terms of my mental equanimity: Would I be fretful and uptight about money, or relaxed and confident?

Framing my quest for *parnassah* this way was life-changing. I still took my responsibilities seriously; I wasn't lulled into inactivity by the knowledge that Hashem was in charge. Yet any time I found myself becoming tense about money, I'd remind myself of the classic words of the *Chovos Halevavos*: "*Mahus habitachon hi menuchas nefesh habotei'ach* — the essence of *bitachon* is the peace of mind of the one who trusts."

I began to give *shiurim* at a local yeshivah on a volunteer basis, and several months later, the yeshivah offered me a paying job as a part-time *maggid shiur*, part-time fundraiser. I felt as though Hashem was telling us, "You see? I had to take away your false sense of security so that I could show you that I'm the One taking care of you."

My father-in-law's remonstrations about our lack of retirement savings notwithstanding, we truly felt that having our IRA wiped out had spurred us to develop spiritual reservoirs that were more valuable than any savings plan.

That didn't mean we were giving up on the $15,000 that Gavriel Klein owed us. The frantic daily phone calls and e-mails eventually slowed down to weekly, then monthly, then yearly reminders. By that time, we understood that there was something pathological about Gavriel's behavior, and that his dishonesty stemmed more from sickness than viciousness. His crookedness had long been exposed publicly, and he had numerous *dinei Torah* and lawsuits behind him.

Still, when he called that Erev Yom Kippur to ask *mechilah* — without having paid the money that would make his apology credible — we were floored by his chutzpah.

"I forgive you for your behavior, and for the *agmas nefesh* you caused us," I told Gavriel. "But I'm not *mochel* the money that you owe us."

I don't think Gavriel will ever understand what a blow he dealt us with his bad check. But in a sense, that check was an unlikely gift — a catalyst that brought us closer to the true, limitless Giver.

To have your story retold by C.Saphir, e-mail a brief synopsis to *lifelines@mishpacha.com* or call +1.718.686.9339 extension 87204 and leave a message. Details will be changed to assure confidentiality.

STUDENT RESOURCE 18

MORTGAGE PAYMENTS & INTEREST

(IN-CLASS EXERCISE)

A. Comparative Table

	30-year mortgage 7% interest	30-year mortgage 4.5% interest	15-year mortgage 7% interest	15-year mortgage 4.5% interest	30-year mortgage 4.5% interest
Loan amount	$200,000	$200,000	$200,000	$200,000	$300,000
Annual interest rate	7%	4.5%	7%	4.5%	4.5%
Loan period in years	30	30	15	15	30
Monthly payment	$1,330.60	$1,013.37	$1,797.66	$1,529.99	$1,520.06
Number of payments	360	360	180	180	180
Total interest owed	$279,017.80	$164,813.42	$123,578.18	$75,397.58	$247,220.13
Total money paid (principal + interest)					

B. Questions

1. What are the advantages of a 30-year-loan over a 15-year?
2. What are the advantages of a 15-year-loan over 30-year?
3. In the last row of the above table, fill in the actual amounts repaid over the term of the loan in each of the four scenarios.
4. Chaim and Devora Schwartz have four children, the oldest of whom is an eight-year-old boy. They need a $200,000 mortgage to buy a house, and interest rates are at 4.5%. They can comfortably afford to pay $1200 a month for their mortgage, but paying $1500 a month would be a strain on their budget, and would require them to tighten their belts significantly. What considerations should they take into account when deciding between a 15-year mortgage and a 30-year?
   - **Inflation** – money is worth less over time, so $1500 gets easier to pay over time.
   - **Weddings** – in 15 years, the Schwartzes will likely have children in shidduchim, and they will probably prefer not to have to be paying a mortgage then.
   - **Higher expenses** – as children grow older and the family grows, cost of living increases dramatically.
   - **Higher income** – as people grow older and become more experienced and established in their fields, their income generally increases.
5. Chaim and Devora decide to stretch themselves to pay $1500/month for a 15-year mortgage. Then, they realize that their car is getting old, and their new house can use some renovations. Of course, they also need furniture. Their mortgage broker offers them a $300,000, 30-year mortgage for practically the same monthly payment as the $200,000, 15-year. If you were in their shoes, what would you do? Why?

STUDENT RESOURCE 19

HETER ISKA FORM FOR LOANS

sample

The undersigned ______________________________("the Manager")

acknowledges receipt of $ ____________________("the Funds")

from ______________________________________("the Investor")

The Manager obligates himself to invest the amount of the Funds on behalf of the Investor in a ny investment or to assign to the Investor a proportionate share of the Manager's assets. If the Manager pays the Investor a return equal to   % per annum on the Funds together with an amount equal to the Investor's usual fees, benefits, and charges for providing funds if applicable (collectively called "the Yield"), and repays the Funds in accordance with and at the times stipulated in the attached Schedule and pays the full amount of the Funds and any accrued and unpaid Yield, to be fully paid to the Investor by the Maturity date __________ , then the Manager shall not be obligated to provide to the Investor any accounting of profits or losses and the Manager shall be entitled to retain all profits in excess of the Yield as the Manager's compensation. The Manager will notify the Investor, in writing, of the amount of the profits or losses on Friday of each week, and in the absence of such notice, the Yield will be deemed to have been earned. If the Yield is not earned in any week, the Investor may call for immediate repayment of the Funds and any accrued and unpaid Yield. The Manager agrees that any claim for loss of any part of the Funds may only be proved by the testimony of two witnesses admissible in accordance with the strictest Orthodox Jewish law before a duly constituted Orthodox Rabbinical Court comprising such rabbis as the Investor may designate in good faith. The Manager agrees that any claim of failure to achieve the Yield shall be binding on the Investor only if the absolute precise amount is proved by an oath of the Manager pursuant to the provision of the strictest Orthodox Jewish law. Such oath shall be of the most onerous of the many forms of oath provided by Orthodox Jewish law, to be taken by the Manager during the course of the reading of the Torah, in such Orthodox Synagogue as may be designated by the Investor, and in the attendance of the Rabbi, the full congregation then in attendance, and a valid Orthodox Rabbinical Court. Failing proof of aforesaid as to the loss of Funds or failure to achieve the Yield, the Funds and the Yield shall be deemed owing as and when due, as set out herein, and the Manager shall be obligated to pay such amounts. Any unpaid portion of the Funds or the Yield shall be deemed reinvested in accordance with the terms of this *heter iska*, both before and after the Maturity Date. This document shall supersede the provisions of any other agreement between the parties which may be inconsistent with this *heter iska*. However, if a Mortgage or other security ("the Security") has been provided by the Manager to the Investor, it shall serve to secure the Manager's obligations hereunder, and the rights and remedies set out in and arising under the Security may be enforced by the Investor in such manner as provided for it in the event of a default by the Manager, subject only to the Manager's right to prove loss of Funds or failure to achieve the Yield, in the manner set out above.

Dated and signed this _________ day of _______ , _______ (year),

in the city of ______________ .

Investor ___________________________   Manager ___________________________

From *A Matter of Interest*, by Rabbi Mordechai Kanner, Targum Press, 2002. Reprinted with permission from the author

STUDENT RESOURCE 20

TAKING CHARITY ON A ONE-TIME BASIS

Question: *I work as a sofer, and I earn a modest income that is usually enough to cover my family's needs on a month-by-month basis. I have never earned much money, but I also never thought of myself as "poor." Several months ago, I injured my wrist, and I was sidelined from work for about a month. During that period, I had no choice but to borrow money from a gemach and from a couple of friends in order to live. Now, I am baruch Hashem able to work again, but I am left with a considerable amount of debt that I do not see how I can repay. A local tzedakah organization is aware of my financial plight, and they offered me a one-time grant to pay off my debts and put me back onto my feet.*

To me, taking tzedakah is anathema, and I would like to avoid it at all costs. But I honestly don't really see any option at this point. I am considering applying for Mesila's services, but because you do not give people tzedakah, I am not sure that you can help me. Is there anything Mesila can do for me?

A: You are to be commended for your reluctance to take tzedakah money. Jews have always gone to great lengths to avoid taking alms, and for good reason. The Gemara (*Beitzah* 32b) says about a person who depends on others for sustenance that the world is dark for him, and that his life is not life. Obviously, taking tzedakah money is something that the Torah views as a last resort, and something that should be avoided if at all possible.

Lehavdil, in the world of economics, evidence abounds that welfare programs actually increase dependency and perpetuate poverty. When people get money for doing nothing, they invariably lose some of their motivation to work for money. This is a psychological reality that is difficult to overcome.

If you were to accept tzedakah, even if only on a one-time basis, you will have crossed the line from financial independence to dependency. And once you cross that line, it will become far more difficult for you to refrain from accepting tzedakah again.

You write that Mesila does not give people tzedakah. It is true that in most cases we do not give out tzedakah *money*, but we actually do give people tzedakah. The highest form of tzedakah, according to the Rambam and the *Shulchan Aruch*, is helping a person become self-sufficient and not need to take money from others. The counseling services we provide put people on their feet while preserving their dignity and financial independence.

In Mesila's ten years of working with families experiencing financial difficulties – and these, by the way, are not limited to "poor" families – we have found that money is not necessarily the solution to financial problems. Financial problems are usually the result of lack of knowledge and poor financial management skills. By helping people to acquire the necessary knowledge and financial management skills, Mesila has helped hundreds of families and businesses to solve their financial problems.

The fact that some tzedakah organizations today are beginning to offer Mesila-style counseling services is an indication that more and more people are realizing that very often, money alone will not solve financial problems. In your case specifically, taking tzedakah on a one-time basis might cover your shortfall for the time being, but it will not prevent a similar crisis from recurring in the future. It also establishes a dangerous precedent.

Let's face it: living from month to month leaves you little financial breathing room, and you could easily land up in debt again in the future. This is not a pessimistic view of your situation; it is a realistic assessment.

If there is a Mesila branch in your community, we encourage you to apply for our counseling services. Mesila can help you develop a budget that will allow you to cover your living expenses, pay off your debts (slowly, if necessary), and save up money for unforeseen expenses or "rainy day" situations such as an injured wrist. (Mesila includes unforeseen expenses in the category of foreseeable expenses. Smart budgeting always takes rainy days into account.)

A Mesila counselor can also help you find ways to increase your income and decrease your expenditures. This will give you the financial breathing room that will allow you to ride out minor financial crises that may arise in the future.

The Gemara (*Berachos* 5b) observes that *"Ein chavush matir atzmo mibeis ha'asurim"* – a prisoner cannot release himself from prison. When people are in the midst of difficult situations, they often are powerless to extricate themselves from their predicaments. This principle is extremely applicable to people going through financial difficulties. Even if you are a financially responsible person, you might find it extremely beneficial to have a resourceful, experienced, and objective Mesila counselor tackling your financial issues together with you.

Before applying to Mesila, however, be aware that our counseling services are far-reaching and very thorough. Helping a family achieve financial stability is not something that can be accomplished overnight, and it takes months, and sometimes years, of counseling before the family becomes fully self-sufficient.

If there is no Mesila branch in your area, then we would recommend that you take the tzedakah offered to you, but that you try to view it as a loan, not as a handout. You can then slowly save up money to repay the "loan." When you save up enough money, you can make a donation to the organization that gave you the money. In this way, you can avoid the stigma of taking tzedakah.

If your local tzedakah organization offers any type of counseling, we strongly encourage you to accept it. These counseling services may not be as comprehensive or as structured as Mesila's, but they are certainly helpful nonetheless.

The Mishnah (*Pe'ah* 8:9) says that if a person needs tzedakah but refrains from taking it, he will eventually be able to support others with his own money. Although this mishnah does not apply to someone who is unable to survive without taking tzedakah, we believe that in your case it probably does apply. If you can find a way out to avoid taking tzedakah, you will reap the benefits of remaining financially independent in both this world and the next.

STUDENT RESOURCE 21

BITACHON & BUDGETING

Question: *Bnei Torah and kollel families receive a certain siyatta dishmaya that helps them to make ends meet in a near-miraculous manner. If they were to begin to budget carefully and keep close track of their income and expenditures, they would likely come to the realization that their finances just do not add up according to mathematical or logical principles. This realization might cause them to leave kollel. It is therefore inadvisable for bnei Torah to adopt Mesila's budgeting practices or become Mesila clients. Instead, they should have bitachon that Hashem will provide for them and not look too closely at their finances.*

A: In his classic work *Chovos Halevovos* (*Shaar Habitachon, Introduction*), Rabbeinu Bachaye states clearly that a *baal bitachon* – someone who relies on Hashem – will be provided for at all times.

The requirement to have *bitachon* and believe that Hashem is the quintessential Provider applies to all Jewish people – members of the workforce and *bnei Torah* alike. It could therefore be argued that for believing Jews, budgeting is a totally unwarranted activity: if a person believes that Hashem will provide for him, why should he have to think about how much he is earning or spending?

The flaw in this argument is that intellectual beliefs and spoken declarations of faith do not a *baal bitachon* make. Rather, the litmus test of a *baal bitachon* is his lifestyle.

True *baalei bitachon* live on an elevated spiritual plane in which material aspirations and physical desires have no place. They are satisfied with whatever Hashem has given them, even if it is the absolute minimum. Regardless of their physical circumstances, they have no fear or worries. They do not need, desire or enjoy material luxuries. Their luxury is living according to Torah ideals while relying on Hashem to provide for them.

These *baalei bitachon* can be secure in the knowledge that they will always have what they need and never be lacking. For them, budgeting is unnecessary.

The Torah does not prohibit people from having more than the absolute minimum. However, people who wish to live with more than the minimum – whether or not they are *bnei Torah* – have an obligation to make sure that they can afford to pay for what they want or feel they need.

People today are bombarded with advertisements, special offers and a dizzying array of available products and services. At the same time, banks and credit card companies offer them instant access to money that is not theirs. How is anyone to withstand these material enticements if not by making careful calculations of their income and expenditures and being aware of just how much they are able to spend?

Some *bnei Torah* and their families are truly *baalei bitachon*, and are capable of withstanding all material enticement and subsisting off the minimum. Other *bnei Torah* do not possess as great a degree of *bitachon*, and are unable to live on a subsistence level.

Bnei Torah and their family members are not required to spurn all luxury – but if aspects of their lifestyle reflect less than absolute *bitachon*, they are required to carefully scrutinize their finances to ensure that they do not spend more than they have.

A person who borrows and does not repay is termed a *rasha*, an evil person (see *Tehillim* 37:21) – not a *baal bitachon*. *Bitachon* cannot be used as an excuse for overspending or lack of financial responsibility. If there is a possibility that a person might fall into debt, he is obligated to budget and do whatever else it takes to make sure he does not incur the label "*rasha.*"

Mesila's assistance involves helping families to develop an awareness of exactly how much they earn and how much they spend. Of the hundreds of Mesila clients who have achieved financial stability, many have been *bnei Torah*. There have been numerous instances where *bnei Torah* switched to better-paying *kollelim* or took on side tutoring jobs after becoming Mesila clients and were able to enhance their ability to provide for their families without weakening the quality of their learning. However, we do not know of a single case in which a *ben Torah* left *kollel* as a result of measuring his expenditures against his income. In fact, many of our clients have reported that their Torah study improved dramatically after they adopted careful budgeting practices.

It is unquestionably true that *bnei Torah* merit a special *siyatta dishmaya* that enables them to devote their energies to undiluted Torah learning. For individuals who are on high levels of *bitachon*, as evidenced by their modest lifestyles and their contentedness with those lifestyles, the *siyatta dishmaya* they receive obviates the need for living with a budget. But for the vast majority of *bnei Torah*, budgeting is not only appropriate, it is a requirement. And when people do what is required of them, their *siyatta dishmaya* is not diminished, but increased.

Part 3:

Assignments

To be used with Unit 1

Assignment #1:
Sources and Questions

Source 1:

דברים ב:ז

כי ה' אלקיך ברכך - לפיכך לא תכפו (ס"א תכפרו) את טובתו להראות כאילו אתם עניים אלא הראו עצמכם עשירים (רש"י).

Question: *Does the Torah want people to flaunt their wealth? Give examples of how showing one's wealth could be a positive thing, and how it could be a negative thing.*

Source 2:

שפת תמים להחפץ חיים פרק ה:

שבתחלה כשהקב"ה מזמין לאדם מעות בחסדו, כדי שיוכל להחיות את נפשו בזה, וגם לפרוע מזה חובות הבורא כצדקה וגמ"ח והחזקת התורה, וכדומה לזה. היצה"ר מסיתו, שעתה נאות לו להתנהג בעניני הוצאות הבית והמלבושים במעלה הגבוה מערכו והפחות כהמכובד, והמכובד כאחד מעשירי העם]. כדי שיתראה לחשוב ומכובד לעיני חביריו. והאדם הולך אחר עצתו, מרגיל את עצמו בזה, עד שבהמשך הזמן הוא נעשה מוכרח לזה להתנהג כדרך הגבוהים.

Question: *How does stretching our lifestyles to have more backfire in the long run?*

Source 3:

א. דברים ט"ו:ח

כִּי פָתֹחַ תִּפְתַּח אֶת יָדְךָ לוֹ וְהַעֲבֵט תַּעֲבִיטֶנּוּ דֵּי מַחְסֹרוֹ אֲשֶׁר יֶחְסַר לוֹ.

כתובות סז:

תנו רבנן די מחסורו אתה מצווה עליו לפרנסו ואי אתה מצווה עליו לעשרו אשר יחסר לו אפילו סוס לרכוב עליו ועבד לרוץ לפניו אמרו עליו על הלל הזקן שלקח לעני בן טובים אחד

סוס לרכוב עליו ועבד לרוץ לפניו פעם אחת לא מצא עבד לרוץ לפניו ורץ לפניו שלשה מילין.

ב. רמב"ם הלכות מתנות עניים ז:ג

לפי מה שחסר העני אתה מצווה ליתן לו אם אין לו כסות מכסים אותו אם אין לו כלי בית קונין לו אם אין לו אשה משיאין אותו ואם היתה אשה משיאין אותה לאיש אפילו היה דרכו של זה העני לרכוב על הסוס ועבד רץ לפניו והעני וירד מנכסיו קונין לו סוס לרכוב עליו ועבד לרוץ לפניו שנאמר די מחסורו אשר יחסר לו.

ג. אהבת חסד להחפץ חיים פרק א:

עוד משמע שם בחינוך, דשיעור ההלוואה יהיה כפי מה שצריך לו להעני, אם ידו משגת. ובאמת כן מפורש במקרא במקום אחר [בפרשת ראה] (דברים טו, ח): "והעבט בעביטנו", וכפי מה שפרשו חכמינו שכרונם לברכה (מכילתא פרשת משפטים פרשה י"ט) דקאי על הלוואה, ושם מסיים המקרא: "די מחסורו אשר יחסר לו".

Question: *"Our extras become our children's necessities" - how is this idea proven in halachah? How can you see from here that sometimes a poorer person is really wealthier than someone with more money?*

Source 4:

רמב"ם הלכות דעות ו:א

דרך ברייתו של אדם להיות נמשך בדעותיו ובמעשיו אחר ריעיו וחביריו נוהג כמנהג אנשי מדינתו לפיכך צריך אדם להתחבר לצדיקים ולישב אצל החכמים תמיד כדי שילמוד ממעשיהם ויתרחק מן הרשעים ההולכים בחשך כדי שלא ילמוד ממעשיהם הוא ששלמה אומר הולך את חכמים יחכם ורועה כסילים ירוע ואומר אשרי האיש וגו' וכן אם היה במדינה שמנהגותיה רעים ואין אנשיה הולכים בדרך ישרה ילך למקום שאנשיה צדיקים ונוהגים בדרך טובים ואם היו כל המדינות שהוא יודעם ושומע שמועתן נוהגים בדרך לא טובה כמו זמנינו או שאינו יכול ללכת למדינה שמנהגותיה טובים מפני הגייסות או מפני החולי ישב לבדו יחידי כענין שנאמר ישב בדד וידום ואם היו רעים וחטאים שאין מניחים אותו לישב במדינה אלא אם כן נתערב עמהן ונוהג במנהגם הרע יצא למערות ולחוחים ולמדברות ואל ינהיג עצמו בדרך חטאים כענין שנאמר מי יתנני במדבר מלון אורחים:

Question: *Why are people influenced by social standards and values? How can a person escape these influences?*

Source 5:

ביצה טז.

כל מזונותיו של אדם קצובים לו מראש השנה ועד יום הכפורים

רש"י

כל מזונותיו של אדם - כל מה שעתיד להשתכר בשנה, שיהא נזון משם קצוב לו, כך וכך ישתכר בשנה זו, ויש לו ליזהר מלעשות יציאה מרובה שלא יוסיפו לו שכר למזונות אלא מה שפסקו לו:

Question: *Our finances are established on Rosh Hashana - so what is in our hands?*

Source 6:

שיר השירים ז יב - יג

(יב) לְכָה דוֹדִי נֵצֵא הַשָּׂדֶה נָלִינָה בַּכְּפָרִים:

(יג) נַשְׁכִּימָה לַכְּרָמִים נִרְאֶה אִם פָּרְחָה הַגֶּפֶן פִּתַּח הַסְּמָדַר הֵנֵצוּ הָרִמּוֹנִים שָׁם אֶתֵּן אֶת דֹּדַי לָךְ:

ספר צרור המור לרב יעקב מליסא

(יב) נצא השדה. אנחנו מבקשים אותך שתעשה אותנו שנהיה משוללי עול הגלות ונהיה כבני חורין בשדה שהוא מקום חירות: בכפרים. שנהיה משוללי עול מזונות רק נלינה בכפרים שנהיה מאוכלי מהן דכתיב ביה דק ככפור. ואז כל חפצך נעשה:

(יג) נשכימה לכרמים. כשנהיה משוללי עול דרך ארץ נשכימה אז לכרמים שהן בתי מדרשות שעל ידי כך נקראים הסנהדרין כרם ביבנה: פרחה הגפן. ואז נראה פריחת הגפן הן התלמידי חכמים שיהיו אז ביתר שאת.

Question: *What are two general social factors that make it hard to learn Torah? How are these two factors different today compared to the last 2000 years of galus?*

To be used with Unit 1

Assignment #2:
Attitudes

Objective:

To examine the differing needs and wants among people from different generations, societies, or backgrounds.

Instructions:

1. Choose two interviewees who come from different backgrounds. (Note: The more different your interviewees, the easier this assignment will be for you.)
2. Develop interview questions (8-10) pertaining to spending attitudes and habits, as well as their decision-making process in their purchases. You may use some or all of the sample questions below, but you must also develop some of your own.
   a. What do you consider a need that others might consider a want? What luxuries can you live without that others might consider a necessity?
   b. How did the society you grew up in shape your personal needs and wants?
   c. What did you lack growing up that you wish until this day that you had had? What did you lack growing up that you feel made you into a better person?
   d. Was there ever a time that you lacked something that you absolutely needed? How did you manage?
   e. What's the biggest mistake you think people make when it comes to spending money?
   f. Can you think of a time that you decided not to buy something even though you had the money for it and it was something you could have used?
   g. What do you think is the best advice a parent can give their child about spending?
3. Write an essay (2-3 pages) on one of the following topics.
   a. Topic #1: Compare and contrast the answers of your two interviewees. How did their differing backgrounds impact their spending and decision-making habits?
   b. Topic #2: "Our luxuries become our children's necessities." Explain this statement, and state whether you agree or disagree with it, using examples from your two interviewees.

To be used with Unit 2

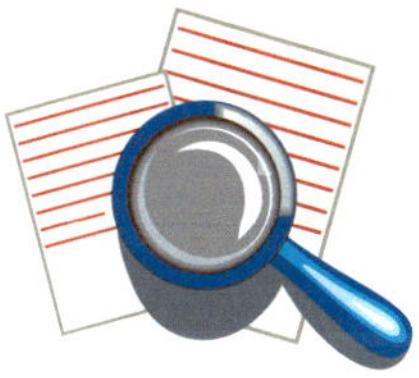

Assignment #3:
Summer Camp Budget

Objective:

To research the costs associated with summer camp and develop a comprehensive yet reasonable summer budget for a camper.

Directions:

Going to summer camp can entail many expenses, both before and during the camp season.

Part I.

1. Camp fees: How much does the camp charge for one month?
2. Shopping for camp: What items will the camper need to buy before camp starts? How many of each item? Be as specific as possible (for example, write "sleeping bag, mosquito repellant, flashlight," rather than "camping gear"). How much will each of these items cost?
3. Camp expenses: Which expenses will there be while the camper is at camp? How much will each of these expenses be?
4. What is the total amount the camper will require in order to meet all of the above expenses comfortably?
5. Suggest four ways to bring down the cost of camp significantly without severely compromising the summer experience. Your suggestions should relate to each of the three expense categories discussed in questions 1-3. (For example: Are the camp fees flexible?)
6. Which of the changes you suggested will be easiest to implement? Which will be the most difficult? Why?
7. How does your camping budget incorporate the rule of "Everything you need and some of what you want"? Give specific examples.
8. Using Mesila's budgeting forms as a guide (see the Mesila Student Guide to Budgeting), create a budget table of camp expenses for your camper.

To be used with Unit 3

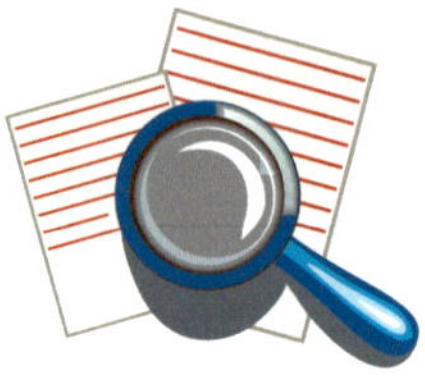

Assignment #4:

Banking Procedures & Services

Objective:

In chart form, compare the banking procedures and services of two banks.

Directions:

Choose two types of accounts (checking/ savings/ CDs) and compare at least three procedures and services offered, and the fees incurred (transfer/ reporting/ receive alerts/ place stop payment / etc.). Create a chart for each bank of your choice.

For example:

City Bank

	Checking Account	Savings Account	Certificate of Deposit
Transfer funds - Possible?			
Transfer funds - Fee?			
Monthly reports - Possible?			
Monthly reports - Fee?			
Receive alerts - Possible?			
Receive alerts - Fee?			

To be used with Unit 3

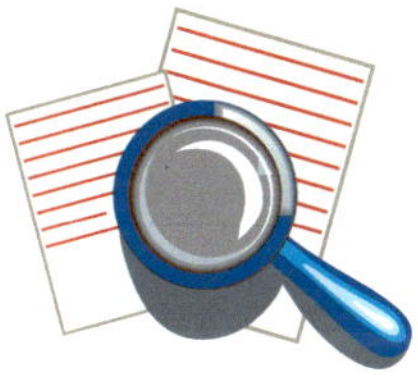

Assignment #5:
You be the Financial Advisor

Mesila's Common Sense Rules for Investors

1. If something sounds too good to be true, it probably is.
2. People who try to get rich quick often lose a lot of money quick.
3. If someone is pressuring you to invest and telling you that the opportunity can't wait, you'd better wait.
4. High returns = high risk. The more money you stand to make, the more money you stand to lose. (If the risks would be low, they wouldn't have to offer such high returns in order to entice people to invest with them.)
5. Bank investments (savings accounts, CDs, etc.) are considered risk-free. Any investment that pays higher returns than the bank is not risk free. But without any risk, you cannot earn more than the bank offers.
6. For every person, there is an appropriate level of risk, depending on how much they can afford to lose. You can take risks only if you are prepared and able to deal with the worst-case scenario (which might mean losing your entire investment, part of it, or having your money tied up for an extended period).
7. "Buy the rumor, sell the news": A hot stock tip that's already public knowledge or is being advertised in the paper is not likely to bring any meaningful returns.
8. Sometimes, a seemingly good investment may be overpriced, which means that you are unlikely to realize any significant returns. A good investment is one that is worth the money you are investing; a bad investment is one for which you overpay.
9. Investments that are based on loopholes or wheeler-dealer schemes are usually not stable investments. Stable investments generally provide some product or service that advances people's needs in some way.
10. Good businessmen and seasoned investors do not need yeshiva students (or the like) to recruit capital for them, and solid investment opportunities are usually snapped up long before they reach the doors of a yeshiva. The types of business deals and investment opportunities that make it through the doors of yeshivos are often the types that are suited to gullible people only.

11. You have more to lose when investing with a friend or relative than with a stranger. With a stranger, all you can lose is money – with a friend, you can lose a friendship as well.

12. Before investing, do your due diligence. That means carefully investigating the opportunity and consulting with professionals and financial advisors regarding the particular opportunity so that you fully understand the risks involved and are equipped to make informed decisions.

This is a situation that a fellow named Sruli presented to Mesila (details have been changed):

Moish, an old friend of mine, recently approached me at the yeshiva where I learn with a very exciting investment opportunity. Moish's father owns an apartment building that is currently being rented to low-income tenants. He wants to renovate the apartments so that he can rent them out to higher-income tenants for double the rent. "Whatever money you invest with my father will triple in under five years," Moish promises. "But you need to hurry! The bank approved financing for this project, but my father needs investors to sign up within 48 hours – otherwise, the financing will fall through."

When I asked Moish whether the plan had any possible risks, he looked hurt. "This is a foolproof plan," he assured me. "Anyone with a little business sense would understand that in a minute. We just need to make sure that we can get rid of all the old tenants and get the building back up to 95% occupancy within six months. But that should be a cinch."

I know Moish well, and he is an ehrliche, reliable person and a capable businessman. Would you recommend that I invest with him?

Part 1.

Analyze the pros and cons of this investment opportunity. Think ahead. What difficulties may Moish and his father encounter with their plan? Does the plan involve any legal or ethical issues or potential pitfalls?

Part 2.

Referring to Mesila's Ten Common Sense Rules for Investors, which rules would Sruli be following were he to invest with Moish? Which rules would he be breaking?

Part 3.

Using your answers to parts 1 & 2, write a response to Sruli's query advising him whether to invest with Moish. (1-2 pages)

This assignment was prepared in conjunction with Mesila's investment advisors.

To be used with Unit 4

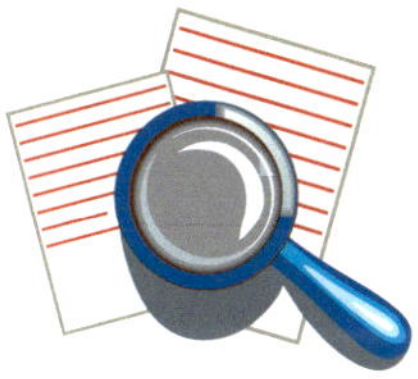

Assignment #6:
Making Informed Credit Card Choices

Assignment: You be the Financial Advisor

Getting a credit card offer in the mail can be exciting. Credit card companies think so, apparently – why else would they send out eight billion offers a year? (That's more than the number of people on the planet.)

But not all offers are created equal. Many people have fallen into the credit card trap and found themselves paying fees they never knew existed. That's why Senator Charles Schumer introduced into law a page of clearly stated disclosures and policies for every credit card. This "Schumer's Box" is now included in every credit card in the U.S.

Before signing up for your preapproved card, with fantastic miles programs and other perks, let's take a look at some different offers and see what makes some cards better than others.

Assignment:

1. Compare the disclosure box ("Schumer's box") of three different credit card offers.
2. What is your introductory interest rate on purchases (APR) and when does the introductory period expire?
3. What happens to your interest rate (APR) if you make one late payment?
4. Does the card have an annual fee? How much?
5. What is the interest rate on cash advances?
6. When does the company begin to charge interest on purchases? When does the company begin to charge interest on cash advances? If there is a difference, explain why it may be significant to the consumer.
7. Is there any circumstance under which the credit card company might change the interest rate?
8. What other factors make one card more attractive than the others?
9. Overall, which card do you recommend, and why?
10. In the absence of the Schumer's box, what information might the consumer have missed?

To be used with Unit 5

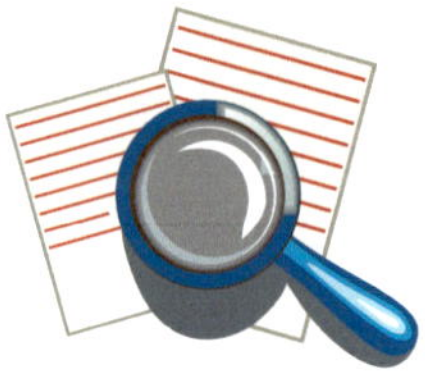

Assignment #7:
Home Ownership Considerations

Scenario

Motti and Dini Hirsch are married eight years, with three children. They are currently renting a 3-bedroom apartment for $1200/month, and they would like to buy a house. The house that they're looking at is in passable condition, priced at $335,000, and is situated on the outskirts of a growing frum community.

Considerations

Location: Right now they are living right near their shuls and schools and near the shopping and a great pizza store. The new house doesn't have such great neighbors…yet.

Repairs: The superintendent takes care of anything in the apartment that breaks. In the ramshackle "new" house, no one is sponsoring the repairs – and there are lots of repairs to be made.

Space: Three bedrooms, one bathroom with three kids is getting a little tight. The new house has four bedrooms, with an alcove that can be used as a study/playroom, an extra bathroom, a bigger living room/dining room and a semi-finished basement that "has potential." There is also a nice-sized backyard.

Financing: The bank will give them a mortgage of up to $235,000, which is 70% of the property value. They have an inheritance of $75,000 from their grandparents. They can borrow $25,000 from relatives and friends to complete the $100,000 down payment.

Payments: Presently, they are paying $1200 in rent. A 15-year mortgage of $235,000 at 5.5% interest will cost them $1900/month, and a 30-year mortgage at 6% (interest rates are usually higher on a longer-term mortgage) will cost them $1400/month. They can manage the 30-year mortgage on their current income, if they squeeze their budget. To be able to afford the 15-year mortgage, Motti or Dini will have to find an additional source of income, but it will take only 15 years for the house to be theirs. They will also have to repay $500/month in private loans for the next four years, which will require them to pay a total of $1900 or $2400/month, depending which mortgage they take – a significant increase over the $1200 rent they are currently paying.

Possible Solution

Motti and Dini decide to go for the 30-year mortgage, and put any extra money they have into their mortgage so that they can pay it off sooner. They can afford the $1400 mortgage, but they need money to pay off the private loans. They decide to buy the house and rent it out. Because the house is a little bit "out," they can get only about $1800/month in rent for it. If they can manage in their current location for another four years, the $1800 in rent will pay their own rent ($1200) plus their private loans ($500), with some allowance for repairs that their tenants will need ($100), while they pay an additional $1400/month for the mortgage. They are also hoping that they will be able to raise the rent on their house, as the neighborhood grows and their location becomes more desirable. Once the private loans are repaid, they can reevaluate.

Alternate Solution

The above solution is one of many possible solutions. Can you come up with an alternate solution to the Hirsch's housing dilemma? Address the above considerations (location, repairs, space, financing, payments) in your solution. Are there any other considerations you think they should take into account? (1 page)

To be used with Unit 6

Assignment #8:

Ethics in Personal Finance

Finances naturally raise many ethical challenges and dilemmas.
Describe and evaluate one such issue.

Directions:

Identify an issue in your community where the value of charity or financial integrity is being compromised. Pinpoint the underlying factors contributing to this issue. Explain and evaluate what is wrong and why it is wrong. How is the compromise of integrity being rationalized or justified? Suggest possible solutions that will rectify the ethical issue without causing damage to the people involved.

Submit answers in an essay format (2-3 pages).

To be used after all units

Assignment #9:

Final Course Assignment
Personal Finance Portfolio & Reflection Exercise

Directions:

Part 1. Portfolio

Select the four written items you have prepared during this course that best exhibit your skills, achievements, and efforts within the course. Present this collection of your work as a portfolio showcasing what you have learned.

Part 2. Reflection and Evaluation Exercise

Describe in essay format (1-2 pages) what you have gained in this course. Use the questions below to guide your reflection (addressing at least four of the questions raised).

1. Which specific point raised in the course was most interesting or surprising to you? Why?
2. What part of this course was the least interesting or relevant to you? Why?
3. What are three things that you will do differently in your own financial life as a result of this class?
4. Which ideas covered in the course will be the hardest for you to implement? How do you intend to overcome those difficulties?
5. "Financial mismanagement can magnify or contribute to virtually any other problem." Explain this statement, giving specific examples to support it.
6. What personal finance advice or guidelines might you give to a friend based on what you have learned in this course? (Your advice should relate to a specific issue in personal finance, such as credit card use, taking loans, or career choices.)
7. How can the skills encouraged or strengthened in this course (such as prioritizing, decision-making, setting goals, accountability, resourcefulness, and delaying gratification) be applied to other areas of your life?
8. Have you shared anything you've learned in this class with parents, siblings or friends? Please elaborate.

Part 4:

The Mesila Student Guide to Budgeting

Table of Contents

A Note to the Student

Dear Student,

Life is not about money, but it sure gets messy when your finances are not in order or you can't live within your means. In theory, living within your means is very simple: spend less than you earn, and you'll be OK!

The problem is that we all have limited money at our disposal, yet there are unlimited possibilities as to what we can do with that money. So the challenge is to use our money in the way that will bring us the maximum benefit and cause us the least financial stress.

Facing this challenge successfully requires a proactive approach: namely, a budget plan. Most people don't like the word budget. It makes them break out into a sweat and think of lots of good reasons why now is not a good time to start budgeting, or why it's not necessary to have a budget.

The reason why budgeting seems so scary is because we tend to associate budgeting with restrictions, deprivation, and stress. People think, *If I have a budget, I'm not going to be able to buy what I want*, or, *If I start budgeting, I'm going to have to worry about how to make my finances work, and they just don't!*

But the truth is that budgeting is not about restrictions at all; it's about giving you **control** over your finances and **freedom** to use your money as you see fit. Your budget doesn't tell you how to spend your money – *you tell your budget how you want to spend your money*. Then your budget helps you to manage your finances in a way that will enable you to spend money on the things you really want.

You might be thinking: Why do I need to learn about this now? I don't have a budget! I don't have finances! I'm only a *bachur*! But surprise, surprise! Now is the perfect time in your life to practice, precisely *because* you don't really have to be responsible for a family budget, which is a really complicated thing, and something that's tough to learn on the job.

Financial management is a very individual thing, and one that every family will approach differently. Nevertheless, having a budget is an important component of financial management **for everyone**. Some people's budgets are so detailed that they leave nothing to chance, and other people's budgets are only basic outlines, but every family needs to have some sort of budget plan in order to stay in – or get back into – the black. When we don't have a plan, we spend more than we can afford without even noticing, and we lose control over our wallets. But with a budget in hand, we regain control of our wallets. And that's a great feeling.

In this guide, you'll learn how to build an effective budget and cash flow plan, and how to avoid common budgeting pitfalls. To make budgeting as simple and straightforward as possible, the step-by-step instructions in the guide are written in clear, easy-to-understand language and are accompanied by frequently asked questions and section summaries.

If you're looking to strike it rich, this program is not for you. But if you're looking for a way to avoid the mistakes that others have made, and control your money instead of letting your money control you, then we hope you'll find this booklet helpful – now, and in the future *b'ezras Hashem*.

Mesila

The First Step:
Establish Needs and Wants

Our goal in budgeting is to allow you to have *everything you need and some of what you want.* That means that you have to know the difference between what you need and what you want. It also means that you have to make sure FIRST that you have what you need, and only THEN see if you can have what you want.

Needs and wants are different for different people. Just because your friend, or your neighbor, or even your older sister *needs* something doesn't mean that you do. And just because they *don't need* something doesn't mean that you don't. That's why you have to get to know yourself, your needs, and your wants.

The purpose of the "Track What You Spend" exercise on the following page is:

1. To take note of spending habits so that we can get to know ourselves and how we spend.
2. To differentiate between needs and wants so that we can prioritize.

Other lessons to be learned from tracking what you spend:

1. For every outlay, there must be a corresponding source of money. (Making that connection may be the most fundamental principle of financial stability.)
2. Becoming aware of your spending habits enables you to identify unhealthy patterns (or patterns that might become problematic later). **Awareness is the basis of all change.**

Let's Get Honest.

(Discussion – in class, or with yourself)

1. How do you define "need"?
2. How do you define "want"?
3. Do the things you want bring you lasting benefit?
4. Which purchases do you regret a week later? Why do you have regrets?

Would a taxi ride to the other side of town (which costs more than a bus but saves an enormous amount of time) be a need or a want, especially when one is on a tight schedule?

Is a much needed vacation a "luxury"?

Does buying take-out food when the Mom works full time constitute a need or want?

Should you buy your 13-year-old daughter a fancy camera that three quarters of the class has?

*When does a **want** become a **need**?*
There are no easy answers!

Track What You Spend!

Date: From____________ to ______________

Purchase	Cost	Source of money	Need or Want?

Let's Build a Family Budget

Here are some straightforward steps for creating a workable budget for a family. In other words: If you were trying to create a budget for your family – and b'ezras Hashem you will, one day – this is what you would do.

Step 1:

Determine the family's income

Start by adding up the family's net annual earnings, including:

- Monthly salary and wages (multiplied by twelve)
- Money from side jobs
- Investment earnings
- Interest and dividends
- Government allowances

If the family has any other sources of income (royalties, rent, parental support, etc.), include those as well.

A word of caution: Do not include possible windfalls – such as gifts or year-end bonuses – in your annual income projection.

If a person has bitachon (faith) that Hashem will provide for him, does he still have to budget?

Mesila actually posed this question to Hagaon R' Aaron Leib Steinman. R' Steinman replied, "If a person would go into a forest without water or food and then collapse, would that be *bitachon*? It would be suicide! Similarly, every person needs to live with a budget and calculate his income and expenses."

Budgeting and *bitachon* are not mutually exclusive. Even a person who has *bitachon* needs to budget, and even a person who budgets needs to have *bitachon*!

Let's Build a Family Budget (cont'd)

Step 2:

Track the family's expenses

To track expenses, write down every dollar the family spends for a minimum of 2-3 months. During this time, hold onto all documentation of the family's financial transactions, including:

- Bills
- Invoices
- Bank statements
- Credit card statements
- Cash register receipts

To keep track of expenses as they occur, keep a paper hanging in a conspicuous place – such as on the refrigerator – to remind you to record your expenses as they happen. Alternatively, you may want to carry a little notebook with you so that you can write down expenses as they occur. If you find it difficult to record expenses on an ongoing basis, you can take a few moments at the end of each day to record all of the day's expenses.

In addition to recording each purchase you make, you need to think about all of the other silent ways that money leaks out of your budget, such as:

- Bank and credit card charges
- Automatic bank account withdrawals
- Post-dated checks
- *Tzedakah* contributions
- Items you buy with pocket change

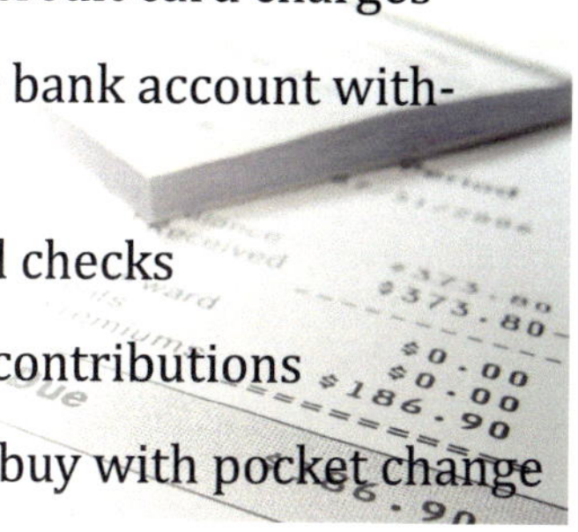

Pay attention to how often you spend small amounts – under $5. **These invisible or seemingly trivial expenses are often responsible for the discrepancy between what you think you spend and what you actually spend.**

Tracking your expenses might be difficult at first, but once you get used to doing it, it will become much easier – and you'll see the benefits very quickly! You'll be amazed at how your increased awareness will put you more in control of your money and help you make smarter spending decisions.

"Yikes! Where did all my money go?"

Has this ever happened to you? You take out your wallet, sure that it's going to be full – but it's empty! *Where did all the money go?* you wonder.

Keeping track of the small stuff is not only for your parents – it can do wonders for your own finances as well. Trivial purchases add up: $2 here, $5 here, and before you know it, that $100 your grandparents gave you is gone.

Try getting into the habit of jotting down what you spend so that you can gain control over your money and use your money in a way that you'll REALLY enjoy.

Should I be tracking all of my financial transactions on a regular basis?

At times, it is necessary to track financial transactions on a daily, item-by-item basis, such as when trying to create a budget and cash flow plan, or when faced with a large, one-time expense (such as a *simchah* or a home renovation). In addition, it is important to track all financial transactions for several months after implementing your budget and cash flow plan, until you are sure that you are successfully following the plan.

Even at other times, you still need to track your financial transactions on a general level to ensure that you are remaining within your budget. But it is not necessary to record every single transaction at that point; reviewing your bank and credit card statements and your check register should give you a pretty good picture of whether you are staying within budget.

If you find it liberating to record all of your financial transactions, since it gives you a sense of control over your money, then by all means, track every transaction. But if tracking your financial transactions down to the last penny makes you feel stifled, then do this detailed tracking only when absolutely necessary. The rest of the time, you can monitor your financial transactions on a more general level.

Step 3:

Calculate the family's expenses

After you have tracked the family's income and expenses for several months, you need to organize the data and group the different income and expense items into general categories. (For instance, group together related expenses such as "taxi ride," "bus card," and "train fare" under a general heading called "transportation.")

Expense categories can be divided into three major groups:

1. Fixed monthly expenses
2. Fluctuating monthly expenses
3. Annual or periodic expenses

Note: When calculating expenses, do not include debt payments (besides the mortgage).

Fixed monthly expenses may include things like:

- Mortgage or rent
- Insurance (life, health, home, auto, etc.)
- Car payments
- Childcare
- Savings plans
- Domestic help

There should be no need for guesswork here, since the amount you pay is usually the same every month.

Fluctuating monthly expenses are a bit trickier. Examples are:

- Food
- Utilities (telephone, cellular phone, electricity, water, gas, etc.)
- Gasoline
- Household products (toiletries, cleaning products, paper goods, etc.)
- Medications
- *Tzedakah* contributions
- Bank charges
- Dry cleaning

These expenses can vary significantly from month to month.

After tracking your expenses for 2-3 months, you should be able to determine a range for these fluctuating expenses. The numbers you will use in your budget should be the ones at the higher end of the range. For instance, if your food bill was $500 one month, $700 the next month, and $400 the next month, you might use $600 as a higher-end estimate of your monthly food costs.

All monthly expenses should be recorded under the month they were incurred, not the date they were paid. For example, if a pipe burst in your house on January 31 and you paid your plumber with a check dated February 28, record the cost of the repair under January's expenses.

Annual and periodic expenses are things like:

- Summer camp
- Medical and dental costs
- Clothing
- Shoes
- Vacations and outings
- *Simchas* and parties
- Home repairs
- Car maintenance
- Travel
- Yom Tov expenses
- Furniture and appliances

Estimate these costs to the best of your ability, using previous years' expenses as a guide.

To determine your total annual expenditure, add up your fixed and fluctuating monthly expenses and multiply the total by twelve. Then add to that your annual or periodic expenses.

Now that you have a fairly accurate estimate of your annual expenditure, pad this figure by 5-10% to allow room for unanticipated expenses. This will give your budget the flexibility to accommodate surprise expenses like parking tickets, lost knapsacks or passport renewals.

After you decide which items belong in which category, we recommend that you ask an objective person outside your immediate family – such as a friend, a neighbor, or a Mesila counselor – to review the items in each category and tell you whether your classifications seem reasonable. This will help you to discover any errors you have made, and may give you ideas for managing your money more effectively. Different families have different spending habits, and there is a lot you can learn a lot from comparing your family's spending habits with those of others.

Mesila's monthly and annual budgeting forms are designed to help you categorize your expenses in an orderly, logical fashion and show you where exactly your money is going.

Step 4:

Compare your income and expenses

Once you have determined how much you are actually spending on a monthly and annual basis, and you have tracked where all the money is going, you can measure your expenses against your income and determine your annual balance using the following formula:

Annual income – Annual expenses
= Annual balance

Now that you know what your annual balance is, you can congratulate yourself on having achieved financial awareness. **Awareness is the foundation for all improvement,** since you cannot fix something if you don't know what is wrong with it. If you and your spouse are aware of exactly what your financial situation is, you will be motivated to take the initiative to do whatever you can to improve it. Therefore, achieving awareness is the critical first step in gaining control of your finances, and is the basis for successful budgeting.

Why do I need to know what my annual balance is?

Your annual balance is *the* most important piece of budgetary information you have. Basically, it tells you whether your income exceeds your expenses, or the reverse.

If your annual balance is positive (which means that your income exceeds your expenses), that is the ideal situation: a surplus. You have extra money to save or use as you see fit, and you do not have the pressure of having to change your lifestyle. You may, however, choose to streamline your budget by "trimming the fat" and eliminating or reducing non-essential expenses. This will give you even more financial leverage and will allow you to put your money to the best possible use.

If your annual balance is negative (which means that your income is less than your expenses), you are running a deficit. Governments have the luxury of operating with a deficit; you do not. Even a small monthly deficit, when accumulated, can easily spiral into out-of-control debt. You therefore have to find additional sources of income and/or think of ways to cut down your expenses.

If your annual balance is zero (which means that your income and expenses are equal), then your budget is exactly balanced. Although on the surface, a perfectly balanced budget seems to be an acceptable situation, it is actually not acceptable, for several reasons:

1. It is almost impossible to calculate *all* of your expenses, so your expenses are probably 10-20% higher than you think. Therefore, if your budget is exactly balanced, you are probably running at least a small deficit.

2. A budget that is exactly balanced leaves you no leeway for unanticipated expenses – and there are *always* unanticipated expenses.

3. If your income and expenses are equal, then you have no possibility of saving for the future (or repaying debts, if you have any). Savings are an integral part of any budget, for they empower you to cope with financial challenges in the future and prevent those challenges from becoming crises. And it goes without saying that if you are in debt, it is critical that your budget be configured in a way that will enable you to repay your debts.

Step 5:

Build your budget plan

Now, you can go on to build a budget plan for the future, taking into account both your current income and spending information as well as future income and spending projections. How you will go about building your budget plans depends very much on whether your annual balance is positive or negative (an annual balance of zero is considered a negative balance, for our purposes).

When building your budget plan, it is critical to ensure that you have a significantly positive annual balance. If your annual balance is negative, or if you already have a positive annual balance but you wish to increase it, you will need to find ways to increase your income or reduce your expenses. The budget forms that you filled out earlier will play a vital role in helping you decide what budgetary changes to make.

Now, take a fresh set of monthly and annual budget forms and fill in projected future amounts for each item, based on the data you have collected and any budgetary changes you have decided to implement (i.e., increases in income and reductions in spending). Also include in your new budget any one-time earnings or expenses that you anticipate in the upcoming months. The projections you write down in this fresh set of forms will become your new budget plan.

Once you have successfully built a budget plan, you can go on to create a cash flow plan that will make your budget plan work for you.

Here are some general suggestions for **increasing income:**

- Learn new, marketable skills.
- Upgrade your professional abilities to make yourself more valuable to your employer and earn a promotion or raise.
- Turn a hobby into an income-generating activity.
- Give private or group lessons to teach a subject or skill that you are good at.
- Work additional hours (possibly off-times, such as evenings or weekends).
- Take on side work in addition to your regular occupation.

Here are some general suggestions for **reducing expenses:**

- Use cash exclusively.
- Look for cheaper service providers in all areas – from your phone company to your cleaning help to your dentist.
- Make a shopping list before you buy groceries, including quantities of each item.
- Don't go shopping when you're hungry, in a rush, or feeling down.
- Buy cheaper generic brands instead of brand names.
- Find creative, low-cost alternatives to expensive family outings.

I want to turn my negative annual balance into a positive balance. How do I decide what budgetary changes to make?

Now that your income and expenses are neatly itemized in the monthly and annual budget forms, you should review each income item and decide whether it can be increased; look for ways to bring in income from new sources; and review each expense item and decide whether it can be reduced or removed. Don't be embarrassed to ask others for their advice when deciding what budgetary changes to make.

But be realistic when making these decisions. Try not to make drastic or sweeping budget cuts, since these typically cause severe stress in the home and are rarely sustainable long-term. Small, localized cuts are usually less painful and more easily implemented.

In general, increasing income is a better way to improve your annual balance than cutting expenses, since the potential for increasing income is theoretically unlimited, and increasing income may involve less stress. It is difficult to plan a budget based on possible increases in income, though, so be very careful when inflating your income projections for the future.

The process of making changes to your current budget often involves much trial and error, so do not be discouraged if your planned budget cuts or hoped-for increases in income do not materialize as you would have liked. If your first attempts at improving your annual balance don't work out the way you would like, keep on trying! You'll get there, with Hashem's help.

Monthly Budget

(Current/Projected)

A. Monthly Income

	Source: Salary/Wages (net)	Amount		Source: Interest/Dividends	Amount	Other Sources	Amount	Other Sources	Amount
Husband			Investment type			Rent			
						Child benefits			
						Unemployment benefits			
Wife						Social Security / Social Insurance			
						Pension/Retirement Fund			

Total Monthly Income

$

B. Monthly Expenses*

Expense Category	Amount	% of Total Expenditure
1: Housing		
2: Food & Household Items		
3: Bills & Utilities		
4: Education & Children		
5: Transportation		
6: Health & Personal Care		
7: Leisure		
8: Miscellaneous		

* See itemized list of expenses on next page.

Space for Calculations

Total Monthly Expenses

$

C. Monthly Balance

Total Monthly Income (end of section A)		Total Monthly Expenses (end of section B)		circle		Monthly Balance
$	−	$	=	+ / −	»	$

Itemized List of Expenses for Section B of Monthly Budget

Item 1: Housing	
Rent	
Mortgage	
Property tax	
Building dues	
Cleaning help	
Outdoor maintenance	
Other	
Total:	

Item 2: Food & Household Items	
Meat & fish	
Fruits & vegetables	
Bread & baked goods	
Packaged foods	
Beverages	
Snack foods	
Restaurant & takeout	
Health food	
Household items	
Paper goods	
Cleaning supplies	
Other	
Total:	

Item 3: Bills & Utilities	
Social Security / Social Insurance	
Telephone	
Cell phone	
Electricity	
Gas / Heating oil	
Water	
Life insurance	
Appliance service contracts	
Bank charges	
Credit card charges	
Interest charges	
Other	
Total:	

Item 4: Education & Children	
School tuition / playgroup	
Daycare	
School transportation	
Babysitting	
Private lessons	
Tutoring	
Baby items	
Pocket money	
Support for single children	
Support for married children	
Other	
Total:	

Item 5: Transportation	
Auto lease	
Gasoline	
Tolls	
Buses	
Taxis	
Carpool	
Other	
Total:	

Item 6: Health & Personal Care	
Health insurance	
Medicines	
Vitamins	
Fitness	
Therapies	
Alternative medicine	
Contact lenses & solutions	
Toiletries & cosmetics	
Health & beauty treatments	
Haircuts	
Other	
Total:	

Item 7: Leisure	
Newspapers & magazines	
Gifts	
Flowers	
Stationery & crafts	
Lottery & raffle tickets	
Entertainment	
Other	
Total:	

Item 8: Miscellaneous	
Tzedakah	
Support for parents	
Savings plan	
Dry cleaning	
Pet expenses	
Other	
Total:	

Annual Budget

(Current/Projected)

D. Periodic Income

Periodic Income	Amount	Comments
Year-end bonus		
Tax refund		
Government benefits		
Charitable assistance		
Gifts		

Reduction of Income	Amount	Comments
Nissan		
Summer		
Tishrei		

Periodic Income $ — Reduction of Income $ = Total Periodic Income $

E. Periodic Expenses*

Expense Category	Amount	% of Total Expenditure
1: Housing		
2: Clothing		
3: Education & Children		
4: Transportation		
5: Health & Personal Care		
6: *Yomim Tovim*		
7: Leisure		
8: Miscellaneous		

Space for Calculations

* See itemized list of expenses on next page. Record only those expenses that are not included in your monthly budget.

Total Periodic Expenses $

F. Periodic Balance

Total Periodic Income (end of section D) $ — Total Periodic Expenses (end of section E) $ = circle + / – Periodic Balance $

G. Annual Balance

Monthly Balance (end of section C on Monthly Budget) $ × 12 $

+ Periodic Balance (end of section F) $

= circle + / – Annual Balance $

circle Adjusted Monthly Balance

÷12 + / – $

Itemized List of Expenses for Section E of Annual Budget

Item 1: Housing	
Homeowner's insurance	
Heating oil/gas	
Home repairs	
Appliance purchases	
Appliance repairs	
Furniture	
Lighting	
Kitchen supplies	
Pest control	
Other	
Total:	
Item 2: Clothing	
Clothing – parents	
Clothing – children	
Shoes – parents	
Shoes – children	
Jewelry & accessories	
Outerwear	
Head coverings	
Shaitel care	
Other	
Total:	
Item 3: Education & Children	
Enrichment for children	
Courses & *shiurim*	
School activities & other costs	
School supplies	
Summer camp	
Day camp	
Other	
Total:	
Item 4: Transportation	
Car insurance	
Car inspection & licensing	
Car repair & maintenance	
Emissions testing	
Parking & tickets	
Shipping	
Postage	
Other	
Total:	
Item 5: Health & Personal Care	
Medical expenses	
Medical equipment	
Dental & orthodontic	
Glasses	
Contact lenses	
Other	
Total:	
Item 6: *Yamim Tovim*	
Tishrei:	
Arba minim	
Succah	
Shul seats	
Yom Tov food	
Clothing & shoes	
Chol Hamoed outings	
Other	
Total - Tishrei:	
Purim:	
Mishloach Manot	
Matanot L'evyonim	
Costumes	
Gifts	
Other	
Total – Purim:	
Pesach:	
Matzah	
Yom Tov food – general	
Wine	
Fruits & vegetables	
Meat & fish	
Cleaning help & supplies	
Dishes & utensils	
Clothing & shoes	
Chol Hamoed outings	
Afikoman presents	
Other	
Total – Pesach:	
Shavuos	
Chanukah	
Tu b'Shevat	
Other	
Total - all *Yamim Tovim*:	
Item 7: Leisure	
Vacations	
Summer residence	
Recreation	
Electronics	
Sports & hobbies	
Toys & games	
Music	
Gifts	
Photography	
Simchas & parties	
Other	
Total:	
Item 8: Miscellaneous	
Tzedakah	
Shul dues	
Aliyos	
Seforim & books	
Computer equipment	
Personal article insurance	
Government documentation	
Other	
Total:	

The Next Frontier: Building a Cash Flow Plan

To keep your finances under control, it's not enough to build a budget. You also need to prepare a cash flow plan. A cash flow plan is simply a way of ensuring that you'll have the money you need, when you need it.

Why is this necessary? Because expenses – and in some cases, income – fluctuate from month to month. Even if your annual budget is balanced and you are earning enough money over the year to cover all of your expenses, you may still find yourself short on cash during peak-expense seasons such as Yamim Tovim or summer vacation.

A cash flow plan will help to ensure that when these peak-expense seasons arrive, you have enough money on hand to cover your bills. It will also help you to determine how much money you need to set aside during low-expense months to carry you through higher-expense months.

For people who do not earn regular monthly salaries, a cash flow plan is even more critical. A real estate agent might earn $10,000 in commissions one month, but nothing for the next two months. A freelancer who does not receive employee benefits might bring home a respectable income during months that have twenty-plus work days, but very little during months that include numerous sick or vacation days. A clothing store owner might post impressive revenues at the beginning of the winter and summer seasons, but have pitifully low mid-season sales. To make matters worse, peak-income seasons do not always coincide with peak-expense seasons; in fact, many self-employed people experience a significant drop in income during peak-expense seasons. (For instance, a musician may not have much work during the Three Weeks, but he still has to pay for his children's summer camp...)

Often, people whose income fluctuates exhibit a "feast/famine" lifestyle pattern, in which they live well during peak-income months, and experience severe financial strain during months when income slows to a trickle. This is extremely stressful, and quite avoidable. To ride out the peaks and troughs of irregular income, you need to develop a cash flow plan that will help you spread your income across the year.

Now that we've discussed budgeting, we will go on to an explanation of how to use your budget as a basis for a cash flow plan.

How do I build a cash flow plan?

When planning your budget, you made proactive decisions as to how you want to spend your money, within the boundaries created by your income. Now that you have a balanced budget, you also have to make sure that you will have enough money on hand to pay for the items included in your budget in a timely manner.

Don't rely on your wallet, or your bank account, to tell you what you can or can't afford. If you listen to your wallet instead of your budget, you're likely to spend money frivolously when your wallet is full and be overly tightfisted when your wallet is empty.

How do you make sure that your wallet is working in tandem with your budget, so that you have the right amount of money at the right time? That's the job of your cash flow plan.

The form entitled "Cash Flow Plan" is designed to help you calculate your projected cash flow and make any necessary adjustments.

In order to build a cash flow plan, you will need to calculate approximately how much money will be coming in (positive cash flow) and how much money will be going out (negative cash flow) during each of the next twelve months.

It is important to realize that **positive cash flow is not synonymous with income, and negative cash flow is not synonymous with expenses**. A person can have lots of income, and yet have negative cash flow – for instance, if his wages are delayed or if his money is tied up in investments and therefore inaccessible. Conversely, a person can have little or no income, and yet have positive cash flow – for instance, if he borrows money or liquidates his assets. (Keep in mind, however, that borrowed money quickly turns into negative cash flow when the time comes to repay it...)

Examples of positive cash flow items: +

- Income that is *paid* (not owed) to you
- Monetary gifts
- Revenue from the liquidation of assets
- Money that you borrow

Examples of negative cash flow items: –

- All purchases and payments
- Automated withdrawals from your bank account
- Money you put in savings or investments
- Debt repayments

Here is a step-by-step guide to building your cash flow plan:

Step 1:
Estimate the timing of annual income and expenses

When you built your budget plan, you differentiated between *monthly* income and expenses and *annual* (or *periodic*) income and expenses. Now, go through your itemized list of annual income and expenses and try to determine in which month each income or expense item belongs. The timing of certain annual budget items (such as holiday expenses, or summer camp) is easy to predict, while other items are difficult or impossible to predict; you do not know, for instance, when you might need to pay for a home repair. Annual budget items whose timing is predictable should be entered on the form under the month in which they are likely to happen.All other annual income and expenses should be added up separately and recorded as "remainder."

Step 2:
Estimate all other projected cash flow for each month

To estimate your projected cash flow for each month, you need to account for all projected positive and negative cash flow during that month. Your cash flow projections for any given month should include:

- Your regular monthly income and expenses
- The portion of your annual income and expenses that you anticipate during that month (which you calculated in step 1 above)
- Any other money that might be coming in or going out during that month (including a portion of your annual remainder, if applicable – see next paragraph).

The remainder you calculated in step one, representing the sum of all annual budget items whose timing is unpredictable, has to be assigned to the various months of the year. You can do this by dividing the total remainder by 12 and adding that figure (one-twelfth of the total remainder) to each month's cash flow figures. Alternatively, you can assign the remainder of your annual expenses to the first two or three months of the year and the remainder of your annual income to the last two or three months to ensure that you are prepared for unpredictable expenses whenever they happen. This money should be put aside in a place that is readily accessible, but not *too* accessible, to ensure that you are not tempted to use it for other purposes.

Obviously, your cash flow estimates will be far from perfect. Unpredictable annual expenses might all happen in the beginning of the year; they might all happen at the end of the year; or they might happen at various times throughout the year. They certainly won't cooperate with your cash flow plan and divide themselves evenly over the twelve months of the year. **Because you have no way of knowing when these expenses will**

happen, the best you can do is give a reasonable estimate. It is therefore important that you monitor your actual cash flow throughout the year and make any necessary midcourse corrections.

Step 3:

Calculate your projected monthly cash flow balance

Once you have those estimates, the next step is to calculate your projected cash flow balance for each of the next twelve months, using the following formula:

Total positive cash flow
− Total negative cash flow
= Cash flow balance

A positive balance in a particular month means that you will have a surplus during that month; a negative balance means that you will have a deficit during that month.

You now have a cash flow projection for the next twelve months.

Step 4:

Make adjustments for negative cash flow periods

Based on your cash flow projection, you can go on to make adjustments to compensate for the period(s) in which you anticipate a negative cash flow.

Adjusting for negative cash flow means finding a source from which to finance the deficit you are anticipating during a given period. If the period in which you anticipate negative cash flow comes after a period of positive cash flow, the best thing to do is to put aside money during the positive cash flow period to tide you over the negative cash flow period. But if the negative cash flow period comes first, or if you are unable to put aside enough money during the positive cash flow period to tide you through the negative cash flow period, then you will need to find an alternate financing source. This source can be either internal (liquidating your own savings, investments, or assets) or external (taking interim loans or credit). In most cases, tapping into your own resources is preferable to borrowing from an external source.

Does it matter whether I start my cash flow plan in a positive cash flow month or a negative cash flow month?

A cash flow plan is meant to empower you to ride out the budgetary fluctuations that inevitably occur throughout the year. Therefore, it is worthwhile to begin a cash flow plan in a position of strength, with cash in hand to tide you through the negative cash flow period ahead, rather than begin the plan with a deficit and constantly have to look back and cover past expenses.

If it is not possible to jumpstart the cash flow plan with cash in hand, however, then it is important to plan *how much* money you will need to cover your negative cash flow, *where* you will take it from, and *how* and *when* you will pay it back. Planning cash flow financing carefully will enable you to borrow or withdraw only the amount you actually need, and ensure that you have a way to repay the loan or replenish your resources.

Cash Flow Plan

A. Projected Annual/Periodic Expenses by Month

In section E of the Annual Budget, you entered totals for each of the eight periodic expense categories listed. Now, calculate what portion of those periodic expense categories can be assigned to specific months and record the amounts below. The portion of the periodic expense categories that is unpredictable should be recorded under "Remainder."

For instance: Most purchases in the clothing category typically take place at the beginning of the winter and summer seasons, so you might assign 40% of your clothing budget to the month of September and 40% to the month of April, and then record the remaining 20% under "Remainder," since you don't know in which month you will incur the remaining clothing expenses.

Month	Projected Expense: Category 1 - Housing	Projected Expense: Category 2 - Clothing	Projected Expense: Category 3 - Education & Children	Projected Expense: Category 4 - Transportation	Projected Expense: Category 5 - Health & Personal Care	Projected Expense: Category 6 - Holidays	Projected Expense: Category 7 - Leisure	Projected Expense: Category 8 - Miscellaneous	Total Projected Expenses: All categories
Month 1									
Month 2									
Month 3									
Month 4									
Month 5									
Month 6									
Month 7									
Month 8									
Month 9									
Month 10									
Month 11									
Month 12									
Total									
Grand Total*									
Remainder (Grand total - Total)									

* Take these figures from section E of Annual Budget.

This is the sum of the projected expense amounts listed above for the 12 months of the year.

Flip back to Section E of the Annual Budget, and transfer to this row the figures listed in the eight categories of the Amount column.

This figure shows the portion of each periodic expense category that is unpredictable. You can't know exactly when these expenses will crop up.

B. Cash Position by Month

In this table, enter monthly estimates for each of the positive and negative cash flow categories and calculate the monthly balance. If the monthly balance is negative, indicate how you plan to cover the deficit by recording the proposed adjustment source and amount.

	Positive cash flow				Negative cash flow								
Month	Projected Monthly Income	Projected Annual/ Periodic Income	Remainder	Other	Projected Monthly Expenses	Projected Annual/ Periodic Expenses (from Table A above)	Savings Plan	Debt Repay-ment	Remainder	Other	Monthly Balance	Adjustment Source	Adjustment Amount
Month 1													
Month 2													
Month 3													
Month 4													
Month 5													
Month 6													
Month 7													
Month 8													
Month 9													
Month 10													
Month 11													
Month 12													

The Final Challenge: Divide & Conquer

The following is an article that appeared in Mesila's Hamodia column.

A Tale of Two Incomes — and a Deficit

Question:

Our financial situation was always such that we never were able to make ends meet. For the first few years after we got married, my husband learned in kollel. We lived very frugally then, but we nevertheless got into debt. When my husband began working part-time, we moved to a different community, where our expenses increased, and so did our debt. We were running to gemachim constantly. Eventually, my husband got a full-time job in a brokerage firm with an income that started at about $25,000 a year (this goes back some twenty years). At that time, the income was inadequate to cover our expenses, and we got ourselves into serious credit card debt.

Over the years, our income has increased. I became a dental hygienist several years ago so I bring home about $3,000 a month, which does help a lot. Our total monthly take home income is presently $10,160, plus my husband's year-end bonus of $10,000.

We still owe a lot of back taxes, and we have a monthly arrangement to pay these taxes. But we often end up buying food with post-dated checks, and we still occasionally get shut off notices from the utility companies. Our financial situation has caused my husband major stress and has really affected the atmosphere in our home.

I'm concerned that we may be really mismanaging our money, since considering our income, we should be managing comfortably. When I list the expenses, though, it looks as though we need several thousand dollars a month more.

Our monthly expenses (not including food, groceries, clothing, yom tov costs, gifts, etc.) are $9,346, itemized below:

Mortgage:	*$2,250*
Property taxes:	*$700*
Gas and electric:	*$600*
Water:	*$80*
Cleaners:	*$120*
Tuition for two children:	*$1,050*
School transportation:	*$230*
Allowance for son learning in Israel:	*$400*
Cleaning help:	*$320*
Pay back on down payment for house:	*$300*
Gemach payments:	*$925*
Income tax (owed from past):	*$350*
Car payments:	*$516*
Car insurance:	*$300*
Gasoline:	*$350*
Homeowners' insurance:	*$125*
Credit card debt (old):	*$250*
Credit card payments:	*$120 (just interest)*
Medicine:	*$100*
Telephone:	*$100*
Cell phones (3):	*$160*

Any help or advice that you can offer would be greatly appreciated.

Mesila's response:

We welcome your inquiry, and we will be happy to assist you to the best of our ability. The situation you describe is all too common, particularly in the U.S.: two parents working hard to earn a respectable combined income, yet struggling to meet their financial obligations.

Mesila's counseling program involves three stages, the first and most basic of which is helping a family become aware of its exact financial situation. You have done an excellent job coming up with a detailed budget breakdown, and we congratulate you on taking this first step towards financial stability. Because you have provided us with a breakdown of your budget, we can hopefully zero in on the source of the problem and offer some suggestions for solving it.

What seems to be preventing you from achieving financial stability is the fact that about 20% of your income is going towards repayment of old debts – not including your mortgage – so you continually have to borrow money to cover your ongoing living expenses.

The way Mesila recommends that you break this vicious cycle is by separating debt from living expenses, using what we call the "divide and conquer approach." Debts and living expenses have to be viewed as two distinct financial obligations and managed as two separate accounts. Your income is meant to cover your living expenses, and your debts have to be paid for from a separate fund.

In the budget breakdown you sent us, debts are lumped together with living expenses and are not itemized. (For instance, when you say "Gemach payments," how many *gemachim* are you paying and how much do you owe to each of them?) The first thing you need to do, therefore, is create a separate, itemized list of debts.

The second thing you need to do is ensure that your annual income is covering your annual living expenses. You have done a good job of itemizing a portion of your monthly expenses above, but it is crucial that you add food, groceries, clothing, yom tov expenses, gifts, and whatever is included in "etc." to your list so that you can determine how much you are really spending. You also need to account for annual and occasional expenses (such as summer camp, or car and home repairs), so that your figures reflect the true annual picture of your finances, rather than a narrow monthly slice of the yearly expense pie.

Once you have accurate figures of your annual income and expenses, you will be able to calculate your annual balance by subtracting expenses from income. If the balance is positive, then you have an annual budget surplus, and you can move on to build a long-term debt repayment plan. If your balance is zero, slightly more than zero, or negative, then you will have to work on increasing your income and/or decreasing your expenditures so that you can carve out a budget surplus, which will become your debt repayment fund.

Whether your annual balance is positive, negative, or zero, you should never use borrowed money to pay for living expenses. Borrowed money includes post-dated checks, installment plans, buying on credit at local stores, and even credit cards, if you are carrying over a balance from month to month. It is critical that your living expenses be covered by your income, to ensure that your debts do not continue to mount. A family that runs an ongoing monthly deficit is headed for financial disaster, so if you find that your income is not covering your living expenses, then you will have to implement emergency measures – which may include working overtime, implementing spending cuts, or even taking *tzedakah* – to close the gap.

We are hopeful, however, that your living expenses *can* be covered by your income, considering that you are earning a very respectable net income of $10,160 a month. Assuming that this is the case, then once you have calculated your annual budget surplus, you can work on creating a fund for debt repayment. This is done by allocating money for all of your living expenses, and then building a long-term debt repayment plan based on your annual budget surplus, which is the amount you can afford to put towards debt repayment every year.

To illustrate, let's say your annual budget surplus is $10,000. If that is the case, you may decide to repay $833 ($10,000 divided by 12) every month. Or, you may decide that you prefer to repay $1,000 ten times a year, so that you do not have to make debt repayments around the times of Pesach and Succos, when your expenses are higher and your income might be reduced. Either way, your debt will be reduced by $10,000 a year. If you find that you can afford to channel more money into your debt repayment fund as time goes on, that is wonderful, but you have to be very careful that paying extra does not result in financial hardship that will lead you to take on more debts or abandon your debt repayment plan because it is too constricting.

In order to create your debt repayment plan, you will probably have to renegotiate the repayment terms of some of the old debts so that your monthly payments can be tailored to an amount that reflects your annual budget surplus. Another option is to consolidate your debt by taking out one large loan to pay off all of the old debts. If you decide to take out a new loan to consolidate your debt, make sure that (a) the monthly payments do not exceed the amount that can afford to repay and (b) the new loan is exactly equal to the amount you owe. (If it is more than you currently owe, your debt will increase; if it is less than you currently owe, you will still be saddled with the burden of repaying multiple debts.)

The advantage of paying back your debts in this manner is that you are able to eliminate your debts as quickly as you can afford to without having to take on any new debts in the interim and without severely compromising your standard of living.

Please realize, however, that the plan that we have just outlined is purely theoretical. To create a realistic, workable plan, you need to invest time and effort to build the plan. As time goes on, you will also need to continually reevaluate your financial situation and your debt load and fine-tune the plan based on your changing financial realities.

Because building – and following – such a plan is challenging, we strongly recommend that you either find someone whom you trust to act as your financial counselor, or apply for Mesila's assistance.

The road to financial stability is often long and arduous, but you seem to be organized, disciplined and motivated enough to succeed in the journey. Feel free to contact us with any further questions.

As we saw in the above article, *A Tale of Two Incomes – and a Deficit*, a common budgeting pitfall is allowing different elements of your finances to get mixed up. In order to really know what's going on and manage your money correctly, you need to differentiate between the following:

Income: Money **coming in** that belongs to you

Assets: Money or property that you currently own

Liabilities: Money that you owe or property that causes you loss

Expenses: Money that you spend as part of your living costs

Maintaining Order – The Divide-and-Conquer Approach

Distinguishing between the many aspects of your finances – which Mesila calls the "divide-and-conquer approach" – is important for two reasons: it helps you to gain an awareness of exactly what is happening with your money, and it puts you in control of your finances by enabling you to make informed decisions.

To implement the divide-and-conquer approach, you should differentiate assets from ongoing income, and debt from ongoing expenses. Loans cannot be considered income, nor can their repayment be considered a living expense. Managing debts and living expenses as two separate accounts will make it possible to get a clear picture of what is going on in each account, and will allow you to achieve control over both accounts in an efficient, orderly manner.

The divide-and-conquer approach extends to other aspects of your finances as well. One-time sources of income have to be differentiated from ongoing or occasional income, and one-time expenses have to be differentiated from your ongoing budget. This ensures that your estimated monthly or annual income is not artificially inflated by a one-time windfall, and that your estimated monthly or annual expenses are not artificially inflated by a one-time outlay.

Similarly, if you have a business, it has to be treated as a separate account. When business and family finances become mixed together, it becomes impossible to reach awareness of what is happening in either one. Separating business finances from family finances makes it possible to reach awareness of what is happening in both, which in turn allows each of them to be managed effectively.

In summary, Mesila uses the divide-and-conquer approach to differentiate between:

- Monthly, annual, occasional and one-time sources of income
- Income and assets
- Living expenses and debt
- Monthly, annual, occasional and one-time expenses
- Business and family finances

Once you have differentiated between these elements of your finances, you will be able to isolate problematic areas from non-problematic areas. Seeing that you are succeeding in at least some areas of your financial management will give you the confidence and motivation to extend your success to other, more problematic areas.

After identifying the areas of your finances that are in need of improvement, you will be in a position to develop distinct strategies to deal with each of those areas.

Financial problems often seem overwhelming, with no solutions in sight. In Mesila's experience, however, even the most complex problems can become manageable if they are broken down into individual, distinct problems and tackled piece by piece.

Divide & Conquer Exercise

The purpose of the following exercise is:

1. To differentiate between the various elements of a family's finances
2. To learn that income has to be designated first for ongoing living expenses to prevent debt from accumulating. (If you use your income to repay debt, you may have to borrow to pay living expenses.)
3. To learn that assets are intended for future or one-time expenses such as buying a home, making weddings, retirement, etc.

Instructions: Categorize each of the items at the bottom of this page into the four categories of the table below.

Income	Assets	Expenses	Liabilities

Bank charges
Bank overdraft
Birthday money
Bonds
Cash
Certificates of deposits (CDs)
Checking accounts
Commissions
Credit card balance
Credit card fees
Debts
Fellowship grant/stipend
Gifts to others

Grocery account
Home
Income tax
Insurance deductible
IRA/401 (k)/RRSP – Canada
Loans owed to you
Mortgage
Mutual funds
Parental support/allowance
Paycheck
Personal valuables (jewelry, etc.)
Post-dated checks
Properties

Property tax
Rent
Retirement funds
Savings accounts
Stocks/shares
Stock dividends
Student loans
Summer residence
Tax refund
Tuition
Tzedakah
Vacations

I have a budget, a cash flow plan, and I've gotten things organized. Now what?

Now that you have created a workable budget and cash flow plan, you need to continue tracking your cash flow for several months until you are sure that your projections are in line with the reality.

About halfway through each month, you should tally all positive and negative cash flow since the beginning of that month. Compare these numbers to your cash flow projections for the month, and see whether you are on target to stay within your budget. If you notice that you are deviating from your budget, now is the time to make a midcourse correction, either by finding a way to increase your income for the month or by spending less than you had planned for the remainder of the month.

If you find yourself consistently deviating from your budget or cash flow plan – in either direction – that is an indication that your budget needs to be reworked. If you are frequently spending more than your budget allows, you may have to recalculate your expenses and adjust your budget to more accurately reflect your true expenses. If you are frequently spending less than your budget allows, you might want to consider upping the amount you designate for savings.

Once you have successfully followed your budget for several months, and you have seen that your income and expense projections are accurate, you may choose to stop tracking your financial transactions on a daily, item-by-item basis. Nevertheless, you should still keep a basic record of how much money is coming in and how much is going out each month, to ensure that you are remaining within your budget and cash flow plan. In addition, when you are anticipating a costly occasion (such as a wedding, or moving to a new home) or a high-expense season (such as Pesach or summer vacation), you should track each expense associated with that particular occasion or season so that you can determine exactly how much you spent. This will help you plan for future occasions, and will also allow you to separate ongoing expenses from one-time expenses so that you can determine whether you have stayed within your regular budget for ongoing expenses.

After your budget is in place and working well, you and your spouse should schedule regular meetings – monthly, or at least quarterly – to assess whether you have stayed within your budget and, if necessary, adjust your budget to reflect your family's changing circumstances.

Long-term Budgeting

Until now, we have been talking about building a short-term budget, which is basically a one-year financial plan that reflects your current income and expenses and also includes provisions for savings (and debt repayment, if necessary).

Ideally, however, your budget should be composed of two parts: a short-term budget and a long-term budget. A long-term budget is less detailed than a short-term budget, simply because it is not possible to make accurate budgetary predictions for the distant future.

To build a long-term budget, you need to look ahead and consider what major expenses you anticipate during the next few years: Do you have a child who is going to need orthodontic work? Are you planning to renovate your house? Are you hoping to make a wedding?

Your long-term budget should include savings for any large, foreseeable expenses during the next few years, and it should include savings for unforeseeable expenses as well. This way, when you encounter an unexpected financial pitfall – e.g., your car breaks down, or you require a medical procedure that your insurance does not cover – you will be prepared. We have to expect the unexpected, because unexpected expenses happen to everyone. The only things that are unexpected about unexpected expenses is *what* they will be and *when* they will happen – not *whether* they will happen.

Your long-term budget should also include provisions for anticipated increases or decreases in income .And if you are in debt ,your long-term budget must include a realistic strategy for repaying *all* of your debts.

How do I know if my budget is *workable?*

In order for a budget to work, it has to be realistic and somewhat flexible. If unbudgeted-for expenses continually arise, or if routine expenses consistently exceed their budgeted allotment, those are indications that the budget is too restrictive and needs to be reworked.

A good budget is one that does all of the following:

- Generously covers all essentials
- Leaves some room for non-essentials
- Makes provisions for unanticipated expenses
- Incorporates both short- and long-term savings

This type of budget creates financial structure, takes the focus in the home off money issues and contributes to an environment in which healthy family relationships can flourish.

Living with a budget requires discipline, but it should not make you feel deprived. If you have indeed created a realistic budget, you should be able to acquire all of the things you *need*, and some – but probably not all – of the things you *want*. Nobody has everything they want, but if you build your budget correctly, you'll be able to have the things that are most important to you, and you should not feel that you are missing much by forgoing the things that you have left out of your budget.

Overview:

Steps of Budgeting

The main steps involved in building a budget and cash flow plan are:

1. Determine your total income.
2. Track your expenses for several months.
3. Group expenses into major categories.
4. Calculate your annual budget balance.
5. Decide what budgetary changes you wish to make.
6. Build your budget plan, ensuring that you have a budgetary surplus.
7. Estimate positive and negative cash flow for each of the next 12 months.
8. Calculate your cash flow balance for each of the next 12 months.
9. Make adjustments for negative cash flow periods.
10. Give your budget a test run, tweaking it as necessary.
11. Continually review your budget and adjust it to reflect new realities.
12. Build a long-term budget.

The following article was prepared by Mesila and published in the Hamodia newspaper.

Taking the Pain out of Belt-Tightening

***Q:** I am choking financially, and I'm hoping that you can help me. I own a store in a large Jewish community, and my revenues have taken a nose-dive as a result of the economic crisis. During the good times, the store profits provided enough for my family to live on, but not much more. Now, however, it is not possible for us to live off the store's profits. I am hoping that business will pick up soon, but in the meantime, my family has had to make dramatic cuts to our standard of living. There does not seem to be anything left in our budget to cut, but even so, we are not managing to make ends meet, and we are falling into debt. Do you have any advice about how we can squeeze our budget further?*

A: In general, the way to cope with any type of financial difficulty is to look for ways to increase income and to decrease expenditures. From your description of your situation, it appears that the steps you have taken to deal with these difficult financial times have been primarily focused on decreasing your family's expenditures. Have you taken any steps to increase your income at the same time, whether by trying to boost the sales in your store or by finding other avenues of income? Have you and your wife brainstormed about ways to supplement the family's income during this recession?

First, Increase Income

The Mesila approach is to focus first on increasing income, then on decreasing expenditures, because increasing income has several advantages over decreasing expenditures.

First, increasing income is a positive, constructive step, while decreasing expenditures is a negative, restrictive step. As such, a family can more easily muster – and maintain – enthusiasm and motivation to increase its income than to decrease its expenditures. Second, encouraging people to increase their income involves no implied criticism of their lifestyle, while encouraging them to decrease their expenditures suggests that they are overspending or spending incorrectly. Third, the potential to increase income is unlimited – at least theoretically – while the potential to decrease expenditures is limited.

We would advise you to make sure that in your efforts to balance your budget, you are expending at least as much effort into increasing your income as into decreasing your expenditures. It is true that in today's economy, increasing income can be very difficult. But that is all the more reason to put effort into it.

Decreasing expenditures does have one important benefit over increasing income, however: it provides immediate, clearly defined budgetary relief, while increasing income takes time and is not always predictable. Along with working to increase income, therefore, it is definitely important for you to look for ways to decrease your expenditures.

The Problem with Drastic Cuts

It is important to note that **the goal is not to drastically reduce expenditures** – even if you and your family are willing to do so – because that will squeeze you into a very tight budget, and Mesila has found that such drastic cuts rarely last. Instead, they create pressure and tension in the home and can cause you to despair and give up on balancing your budget.

Even minor spending cuts can result in tension between spouses and between parents and children. When people have to get used to living with less than they are accustomed to, it hurts, especially in the beginning. For that reason, we urge anyone who is trying to reduce spending to do it in a way that will cause the least pain to the family.

The approach that we recommend turns reducing expenditures into a positive exercise, rather than a negative one. In this approach, the goal is not to cut corners, trim the fat, or tighten your belt – the goal is to optimize your spending and build a brand new spending budget tailored to your family's needs. Instead of focusing on your past spending habits and seeing what you can cut, you will erase all of your spending history from your mind and come up with creative ways to meet your needs cost-effectively.

The way you have been spending money until now is definitely not the only way to meet your family's needs, and it is probably possible for you to meet those needs just as well – or better! – while spending less money. In fact, even if you would not have an urgent need to decrease your expenditures, it would be a good idea to periodically rethink your spending patterns and determine how you can get the most value for your money.

Building Your New Spending Plan

When you sit down to make a new spending plan, keep your mind open to all possibilities. Do not accept anything you have done until now as a given. What you have done in the past, and what your friends, relatives and neighbors are doing, is only marginally relevant during this exercise.

Your new spending plan should itemize all of your family's needs – from housing to dental work to keeping the children occupied during summer vacation. But it can involve major changes to the way you are meeting those needs. To illustrate: the housing market is down right now, so you may be able to renegotiate your rent or mortgage payments, or even move to a different house, at considerable savings. Your dentist might be an old friend whom you have been going to for years, but other dentists may do work that is equally good – at better prices. And you might not have to spend thousands of dollars to make summer vacation an enjoyable time for the whole family.

When building this new spending plan, do some research about the different options available to you, and don't be afraid to think out of the box. In addition, do not hesitate to switch any type of service provider, whether it's your phone company, your bank, or your insurance agent.

Plug the Leaks

Although you are erasing your old spending habits and building a spending plan from scratch, it is still important to examine your past and present spending patterns. These old spending patterns should not serve as a guide for building your new spending plan; they are important mainly for their research value.

Reviewing your spending will give you valuable information as to what your family's needs are, and will alert you to the many areas of your budget that you should reassess. It will also help you to see where money is leaking out unnecessarily.

You and your wife should track your expenditures for a period of two to three months. After that, you should prepare an itemized list, broken down into categories, in which you will tally how much you are spending on every item of your budget, from vitamins to haircuts to credit card fees. Then you will be able to evaluate which of these expenses can be eliminated or reduced. This exercise can save you a great deal of money, much of it painless.

Think Before You Spend

You will likely find that just the act of recording your expenditures results in significant savings. Having to write down what you are spending prods you to think before you spend, and thinking is one of the greatest money-saving tools available.

So much of the money we spend happens thoughtlessly – we buy a snack on the road when we could easily have taken one from the house, we pay late fees on bills that we simply forgot about, or we run to the hardware store to buy a tool when we have the identical tool sitting on a shelf in a storage room. By training ourselves to think before reaching into our wallets, we can bring ourselves significant budgetary relief.

Focus on Big-Ticket Items

When cutting expenses, people often focus on budgetary items that are relatively trivial ("No more candy! No more art lessons! Shut the lights!"), while overlooking the big-ticket items that comprise the lion's share of their budget. Things like rent or mortgage payments, insurance premiums, and car payments are huge expenses, and it is in those areas that spending cuts can provide the greatest financial relief.

At the same time, however, it is important to remember that every drop adds up, and every little bit that you save is significant. Your budget contains hundreds of small items, and when added up, these small items amount to a considerable percentage of your spending.

Another important aspect of streamlining your budget is ensuring that you are receiving any discounts, tax breaks and government benefits that you are entitled to. As a small business owner, you may be eligible for certain types of assistance, and we recommend that you speak to a competent accountant about this.

What Works for You

The challenge of decreasing expenditures is to streamline your budget without compromising the family's physical and emotional wellbeing. This challenge is highly individual, for one family might feel deprived living with something that another family is perfectly satisfied with. For instance, one family might have no problem buying generic or store-brand products – from detergent to breakfast cereal to clothing – while another family might find it very difficult to abandon the brand names it is accustomed to. Which family is right? It's not a question of right and wrong. It's a question of what works.

If you are willing to think creatively and reprogram your family's spending habits, you may be pleasantly surprised to find that your budget can go a lot further than you thought.

The following article was prepared by Mesila and published in the Hamodia newspaper.

Before You Throw in the Towel on Budgeting

***Q:** My family would probably be described as a typical middle-class family. Our income is decent, but not great, and our expenses are close at the heels of our income – too close for comfort, probably, but no worse than most other families. Our home is not in danger of foreclosure, so we can't be doing that badly, considering the crisis.*

I've been following your column for some time now and I've actually tried implementing much of your advice. I tried sitting down with my wife and building a budget plan, but it was a dismal failure. We decided to record all of our expenditures so we could see where our money was going, but we just could not remember to write everything down, so that attempt petered out after a few days. The first month of our new budget plan, we ended up spending so much more than we had planned and buying so many things that weren't included in the budget that we just gave up on budgeting. We also tried starting to put aside money for savings – and this something we both really wanted to do – but when our washing machine broke suddenly it wiped out all of our newfound savings and we just couldn't manage to get the savings habit started again.

No matter how many times I try to manage my finances the way I would like to, I always find myself falling back into the same old patterns, the same old problems, time after time. I was about to resign myself either to the fact that I am not cut out for budgeting, or to the fact that I just don't have enough time to be busy with it, but before I threw in the towel on budgeting I thought I'd ask you why I'm having such a hard time with this.

A: Your question is one that we are sure everyone can relate to on some level. Financial management can be very frustrating, and it can be very tempting to let go of the financial steering wheel and allow your finances to coast along on their own. The problem is that the path to financial stability is strewn with hazards, and navigating that path on cruise control can lead you into a tailspin of debt, dependency and unbearable stress.

Financial management today is a complex, bewildering task, one that requires a combination of strategic planning, self-discipline and persistence. For some very disciplined people, financial management comes easily, but for most people, it is a difficult and frustrating task. That's why even bright, capable people like you feel they are "not cut out" for budgeting.

Financial management wasn't always as hard as it is today. In the not too distant past, money was something you carried in your wallet or kept under the floorboards. If you wanted to buy something – and there wasn't that much to buy – you took out a few coins or bills and never had to think later about how to pay for it. If you didn't have the money to buy what you wanted, you either did without or scrimped and saved until you had the money for it.

Back then, money was something tangible, not a bunch of abstract numbers on a bank statement. Budgeting was a straightforward task: you counted your money, and then allocated it for the things you needed the most. You also tried to put something aside for a rainy day, so that you would not have to go hungry if your source of income dried up.

Many people ask us why there is a need for an organization like Mesila nowadays, since "Our grandparents managed just fine without Mesila." Indeed, our grandparents did not need Mesila – they had Mesila in their bones, and living without a budget was unthinkable to them. They also were not under continuous bombardment by a multibillion-dollar advertising industry hawking the wares of the global marketplace and modern technology, nor were they at the mercy of banks and credit card companies offering "attractive financing options" to pay for all that the 21st century has to offer.

Mesila started out in 1998 as an organization that helped people in Israel who were in debt and could not get their finances under control. But in the process of helping hundreds of families and businesses work towards financial stability, we realized that financial management difficulties transcend geographic and socioeconomic divides, and almost everyone today needs help managing their finances. That was why three years ago we shifted our focus to education and prevention, instead of crisis intervention.

The economic crisis we are now experiencing is the result of poor financial management at every level, from corporate bigwigs all the way down to the little guy with the big mortgage. We believe that the answer to this crisis is not dramatic government bailouts, but old-fashioned self-discipline and careful budgeting.

Thankfully, you are still a step ahead of the crisis. But that is much too close for comfort. You are lucky that you had some savings to tide you past a broken washing machine, but what would happen if your boiler went? We are not trying to be pessimistic, but we think that burying your head in the sand and hoping that things will work out is not optimism, but poor planning. You need to be aware of what is going on with your finances, you need to establish financial goals for the future, and you need to create and follow a budget that will help you realize these goals. The other option is financial mayhem, which in the worst-case scenario leads to disaster, and in the best-case scenario leads to putting out fires.

What does "putting out fires" mean? It means discovering all of a sudden that your bank account is overdrawn and having to face all the people to whom you wrote bounced checks. It means paying 20% interest on your credit card balance until you come up with "extra" money (we've never actually heard anyone say they have extra money) to pay it off. It means waking up in middle of the night and remembering that you don't have the money your daughter needs in the morning to pay for her school trip. And it means living a life of balance transfers and debt juggling, borrowing money from one source to repay a loan from a different source.

If correct financial management is difficult and time-consuming, poor financial management is infinitely more difficult and time-consuming. The difference is that correct financial management requires you to exert yourself and exercise self-discipline ahead of time, while poor financial management allows you to take the path of least resistance and suffer the consequences later. Although this path is ultimately the harsher one, it is the default route and therefore the one more trodden.

Like you, many people tell us that they don't have time to create, follow and review their budget plans on a regular basis. That's a bit like saying that you don't have time to look both ways before you cross the street. If you think that analogy is exaggerated, that is because you haven't spent as many hours as we have helping families to extricate themselves from financial crises that could have been avoided.

We don't want you to become one of those families, and that's why we are trying to help you understand that correct financial management is not just a nice bonus; it's a necessity. The investment of time and effort now to create and follow a budget can spare you a tremendous amount of time and frantic effort later to come up with money to pay for sudden (or not-so-sudden) expenses.

Besides for preventing financial difficulties in the future, correct financial management has tremendous positive benefits. Having your finances under control will reduce the amount of financial tension in your life, which will in turn make you a more relaxed person and therefore a better husband and father. If your finances are being managed correctly, you will have an easier time concentrating during your davening and Torah learning, and you will be free to pursue your livelihood to the best of your ability without feeling like a slave to your *parnassah* worries.

Living with a budget is emancipating, for it allows you to truly enjoy everything Hashem gives you without having to worry about whether you can afford it. Although it may require you to give up certain comforts or conveniences, living with a budget will bring you peace of mind and security, which will make every moment of your life sweeter. Shlomo Hamelech says as much when he tells us that a piece of dry piece of bread that has peace in it is better than a banquet where tension and strife reign (*Mishlei* 17:1).

Correct financial management compels you to look inward and make decisions based on what *you* need, what *you* can afford, and what is important to *you*, instead of looking outward at what the neighbors have and wondering how they can afford it. Focusing on your neighbor's Lexus will never bring you any happiness, but focusing on what *you* really want out of life will. By forcing you to clearly define your priorities and goals, a budget can help you to manage your money in the way that will bring you the maximum satisfaction out of life.

Understanding the benefits of correct financial management is the best way to motivate yourself to muster the self-discipline and persistence to track your expenditures, stick to your budget plan, and save for the future. Your wife also has to be convinced of the benefits of correct financial management, since the slightest resistance on her part can torpedo your efforts.

Once both of you are convinced of the benefits, the next step is to develop a system of financial management that works for you. You might have to experiment with a few different approaches, but if you persist, we are sure that you can find the approach that is right for you.

Here are some practical suggestions for coping with the specific issues you mentioned:

To track your expenditures successfully, keep a small notebook with you at all times to record expenditures as they happen, and save all of your receipts, bills and bank statements.

To ensure that you stick to your budget, schedule specific times when you and your wife can sit down alone to review your budget and make any necessary changes. You and your wife are teammates, not adversaries, and your "budget meetings" should be calm, pleasant discussions. These meetings are the time for you and your wife to communicate any concerns you may have and to look for ways to address those concerns. Decisions made at each of these budget meetings should be written down, since writing down budgetary information contributes to financial control and discipline.

To strengthen your resolve, you can read Mesila's articles and other materials, use our budget questionnaires, or attend a Mesila financial management workshop. (If you wish to organize a workshop series in your community, please contact us and we will try to arrange it.) Being part of the Mesila movement can turn financial management into a rewarding experience, instead of a pain in the neck, and can give you the tools and enthusiasm to take control of your finances in a lasting way.

Contentment

"Who is wealthy?
He who is content with his lot."

(*Mishnah, Avos* 4:1)

Many people mistakenly think that in order to be wealthy, you need to have a lot – a lot of money, a lot of possessions, a lot of property. But the Torah teaches us that if you are content with *your* lot, you are wealthy. Having more just makes you want even more, as the Midrash says, "One who has a hundred, wants two hundred" (*Koheles Rabbah* 3:1). A home where the atmosphere is one of contentment is a rich, happy, and healthy home.

Discontent is the archenemy of financial stability, for it leads people to want and need more and more and more. But no amount of material acquisition can drive away the feeling of discontent and bring a person lasting happiness. That is because the root of discontent is in the soul, which thirsts for spiritual fulfillment (*Koheles Rabbah* 6:6). "The soul cannot be filled," King Solomon tells us (*Koheles* 6:7), for it does not accept the currency of the physical world. Money and earthly pleasures are like salt water to the parched soul; instead of quenching the soul's discontent, they intensify its yearning for the true pleasure of closeness to G-d.

The understanding that it is not money or possessions that bring happiness can go a long way in helping you to exercise financial restraint and self-discipline. If you know that material acquisitions are but cheap substitutes for true fulfillment, you will find it much easier to stay within your budget and keep your finances under control.

From the Mesila 12-Point Guide
to Financial Stability

Made in the USA
Las Vegas, NV
03 November 2026

57424223R00112